Share Jesus

with a

Friend

Share Jesus

with a

Friend

Mark Hikes

ISBN 978-1-934817-55-1

by Mark Hikes

10 9 8 7 6 5 4 3 2 1

First Edition

GAP

Great American Publishers

171 Lone Pine Church Road • Lena, MS 39094
TOLL-FREE 1.888.854.5954 • www.GreatAmericanPublishers.com

To purchase books in quantity for church groups,
corporate use, incentives, or fundraising, please call
Great American Publishers at 888-854-5954.

Attention Youth Leaders... if you use this with your group,
we would love to hear from you. Call or text Mark Hikes with
your feedback or to talk about having him visit your youth group.
(717) 439-8575 or mhhikes@gmail.com

Table of Contents

Foreword

For the past six years I have been blessed to be Mark Hikes' pastor, so I was very aware of his ministry to some of our students which was the basis of his first book, *15 Minutes with Jesus*. I hope you will read and practice the things that Mark shares here because it has so much to say about Christian discipleship.

First, this book will help you grow in your own discipleship. Mark gives a lot of attention to abiding in Christ and to the spiritual disciplines of the Christian faith. Whatever God calls us to do for Him, it comes from the growing and transforming relationship that we have with Him. Mark would not want any of us to go out and "do" for God without first having that kind of relationship with Jesus and this book will share ways in which we can do that.

But Mark then makes sure to highlight a critical part of discipleship that we too often miss, that all are called to be disciples and that all of us are to then make disciples. So many well-intended books about discipleship seem to be a bit self-centered by raising questions like, *What new insight can I learn?*, *What does God want me to have?*, or *How will God fill me and change me?* Jesus does not model and call for a pattern for discipleship of only learning and following. We constantly see His compassion for those on the "other side" (Mark 4:35, 5:1, 6:45, 8:13) of faith who need His saving grace and then Jesus commissions and sends His disciples out to reach them. Following Jesus' pattern, discipleship is not complete until we are making disciples. Mark calls it a "MUST" and shares practical and insightful ways for his readers to grow in sharing the Gospel with others. Our growth in Christ, the focus of his first book, has to produce a fruitfulness in our "next 15 minutes" of disciple-making.

Another reason I am honored to speak to this text is because of the hours I have spent with Mark sharing in his life and ministry. He rightly reports in this book that its purpose is "to bring glory to God - not the disciple." Yes, may that always be so! But I do want to say that I have watched Mark be vulnerable about his faith and he does that in this book multiple times. He admits struggles of when he does "fall short," or when he has not "fully...surrendered (a) part of his life." Any form of evangelism that does not contain humility will not honor Jesus and will deter those who do not know Jesus.

Part of my enthusiasm for this book is because I have witnessed how Mark has faithfully lived out the things of which he writes in it. This book not only comes from his heart for others, but it is how he actually lives with others. He writes in this book that we should "tell EVERYBODY" about Jesus and Mark really does that. He intentionally and routinely shares Jesus with his family, with his friends, and with strangers. There are solid biblical principles for evangelism in this text and you will want to take notes on the practical "how-tos" as well as the warnings that Mark gives about how we share our faith. But much of what he suggests comes from just living it out and sharing Jesus consistently and naturally with others. I have always listened to and have given more attention to advice from people who live out what they were sharing.

I am excited for what God will do in you and through you due to your next 15 minutes of interacting with each reading. My hope is that this book will encourage you and remind you of what we can have in Jesus as well as call you to, and equip you for, the great ministry and mission of making disciples for Jesus Christ.

Rev. Dr. Barry Male, Jr.
Senior Pastor
Madison United Methodist Church

Preface

If you have not already read it, *15 Minutes with Jesus* was inspired by my love for an incredible group of 10th graders. It was inspired by my desire to share in their Christian journey. It simply started by me wanting to stay connected with them on a daily basis and help them, with their walk with Jesus. Little did I know how much the group would help me.

These students ask amazing questions which start great discussions that I don't always have the answer to. At first that was a little intimidating! But, it made me grow. It made me want to be better for them. Now, as we continue our walk, I want to talk to you about "the next 15 minutes." Let's share Jesus with someone else! This book can and will be read as a devotional to help you on your journey, but the theme of the first week is discipleship for a reason. It is important for all of us to share Jesus with others. So, as you read each day in this book, think about how you can share the day with someone else.

Sometimes, when I speak to others about the importance of sharing Jesus, the conversation can get quiet. I'll get responses like, "Mark, I just don't know enough." "I just don't feel comfortable." "I get really nervous and I don't want to mess up." My response is always the same... I know what all that feels like.

Several years ago, I met up with Jesus. After finding Him, my life changed forever. Having a relationship with Him has been amazing. It wasn't too long after accepting Him into my life that I had this nudge... to do more... to share Him. And I've been doing it ever since. Trust me it wasn't easy at first. I thought I had to be an expert, but quickly realized that I was not. Admitting to someone that I didn't understand something? Well, I just couldn't do that. Then I realized the reason for this issue... we are "wired" to think we have to have the answers for everyone, on everything, all the time:

- As kids we want to... need to... have answers for our teachers.
- As parents, we want to have answers for our kids.
- As employees, we want to have answers for customers, and we better have them for our bosses.
- As bosses, we must have answers for our employees.

So, as you can see, as we progress through life, every stop requires us to either want answers or be the answer guy/girl. It can be so difficult to admit we don't know stuff.

Many people view it as a credibility sort of thing. Lucky for me, I've never been worried about that. If I don't know something, I'm going to gain knowledge in that area of my life. I discovered that if I wanted to share Jesus with others, I needed to spend more time with Him myself. As my relationship grew deeper, I realized we have a lot of work to do. But I also realized it is not work, it's a privilege. As we walk with Jesus, we get to do many things:

- We get to spend time with Him daily.
- We get to learn from Him.
- We get to teach others about Him.
- We get to be kind to others and love others.
- We learn to be better friends, better siblings, better parents, better spouses and more engaged disciples.

We get all of those things because of the amazing example Jesus lived for us.

Still nervous about sharing Him? Here's what I want you to do for me. Think about the time when you decided that you wanted to ride your bike without those training wheels. I can still remember my dad telling me, "Once I take them off, they're staying off." I didn't care! I wasn't scared! Let's do this! Well, it didn't go to well! I just couldn't keep my balance. My dad could see how much I wanted this... how hard I was trying. So, you know what he did? He put his hand on my shoulder and helped me keep my balance. It didn't take long, and I was keeping my balance on my own. Well…. That is what discipleship is like. If you really want to share Jesus, He will be right there with you... helping you learn and share His story. He loves us so much.

Let's make sure everyone knows about our AMAZING friend! It doesn't take a lot of time. It may take more time with some people than others. But fifteen minutes will be a good start.

Let's get started!!

Discipleship

Am I a disciple? How do I do that? Well let's see what Jesus said about that.

Matthew 28, 16-20, is known as *The Great Commission*. Jesus has risen from the tomb, and the disciples have gathered to meet with Him. Close your eyes, put yourself there. Think about what they must have been feeling. Their Teacher, their Mentor, their Friend that they have spent about 3 years with, had been put to death. And now, He is standing in front of them talking to them. Now Jesus has given some of them proof before this meeting, but my guess is that some of them may have been seeing Him for the first time here.

Jesus' command was not only intended for His first disciples, but also for us today. He says "go and make disciples." The word go, shows us that discipleship requires action on our part. We all may have different roles. We all have different things we are good at. There are so many ways we can share the love Jesus shows us, with others. Discipleship looks different, depending on the need:

Maybe it's a person who's never heard about Jesus

Maybe it's a friend, who needs a reminder

It could be a hug for a person who needs it, or a listening ear for someone who needs to talk.

All of us can have a part in telling others about our AMAZING friend Jesus. Discipleship can be serving that we do "somewhere". I refer to that as "on purpose" scheduled time. But as you can see from those few little descriptions, discipleship can also be a spontaneous encounter. That is why it is so important to be ready to share Jesus all the time.

How important is sharing Jesus, in my life?

Matthew 28 16-20

Then the 11 disciples went to Galilee, to the mountain where Jesus had told them to go. When they saw Him, they worshiped Him; but some doubted. Then Jesus came to them and said, "All authority in heaven and on earth has been given to me. Therefore go and make disciples of all nations, baptizing them in the name of the Father and of the Son and of the Holy Spirit, and teaching them to obey everything I have commanded you. And surely I am with you always, to the very end of age."

Who were the first disciples? What does it take to be a disciple? How long did it take them to decide to follow Jesus?

Matthew 4, v.20, is pretty impulsive. Should we view this as a model for discipleship? Let's go! We can ask questions along the way? Some commentary I've read suggests that Peter and Andrew may have followed Jesus in a limited sense before this encounter. If that was the case, then they had already seen Jesus' power and were ready for the "all in" commitment!

These men dropped everything and followed Jesus. This invitation from Jesus was not an offer of salvation, but to go to work with Him. They had to give up everything, even their cell phones (got you 😄) to follow Him. They did all of this for an uncertain future of winning souls.

They were just ordinary men. No degree in Ministry, just the call that Jesus made to them. These two men were just the first of an elite 12, that through Jesus, with Jesus would make a GIANT impact on the world.

I wanna be part of that team!! How about you?!

What are some ways that God may use me?
Am I willing to share Jesus?

Matthew 4: 18-20

As Jesus was walking beside the Sea of Galilee, he saw two brothers, Simon called Peter and his brother Andrew. They were casting a net into the lake, for they were fishermen. "Come follow Me," Jesus said, "And I will send you out to fish for people." At once they left their nets and followed Him.

Let's add a little bit to yesterday. So, we have two fishermen and a few other disciples. Simply ordinary people. But can anyone be a disciple?

Tax collectors were a group of Jews hated by other Jews for teaming up with the Roman Government that ruled over them. They paid the government for the privilege of collecting the tax then overcharged the people. The people saw them as thieves and traitors. So, needless to say, Matthew was not a very popular guy, yet Jesus wanted him.

So, the answer is YES! Anyone can be a disciple. Jesus doesn't care about your past. If you ask for forgiveness and accept Him into your heart you can disciple others!! He loves us so much. Our sins are forgiven because of Him. All Jesus really cares about is what is in our heart!!

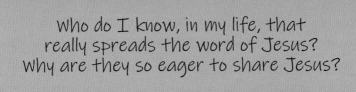

Who do I know, in my life, that
really spreads the word of Jesus?
Why are they so eager to share Jesus?

_____

_____

_____

_____

_____

_____

_____

_____

_____

_____

_____

Matthew 9:9-12

As Jesus went on from there, He saw a man named Matthew sitting at the Tax Collectors booth. "Follow Me", He told him, and Matthew got up and followed Him.   While Jesus was having dinner at Matthew's house, many tax collectors and sinners came and ate with Him and His disciples. When the Pharisees saw this, they asked the disciples, "Why does your teacher eat with tax collectors and sinners?"   On hearing this, Jesus said, "It is not the healthy who need a doctor, but the sick."

As disciples of Jesus we better walk the talk. That is His expectation. Paul suggests the same thing in his letter to the Christians in Corinth.

In the last few verses of chapter 10, Paul is talking about the fact he has the free will to do anything he wants to do. But, not everything is beneficial. Not everything is good. Not everything is ok.

If and when we decide to become a disciple of Jesus, we definitely need to start living differently. We need to strive to be Christ Like. That is a very tough task! We are surrounded by the opportunity for sin. There are things and people in our lives that will be distractions, pulling us away from being Christ like. But there will also be people in our lives that will help us and even join us. That is an extremely important part of my message to you. Surround yourself with good people.

Here are a few questions to ask yourself.

- Will what I'm doing, glorify God?
- Will what I'm doing build up my neighbors?

Paul is telling the people of Corinth, follow my lead, as I follow the example Jesus showed me. The key message / question of this passage is; what are our intentions? They are more important than anything we give up to spend time with Jesus.

So, as we begin to tell others about Jesus, we better be walking the talk, because everyone is watching.

What am I doing in my life that makes my relationship with Jesus, highly visible?

1 Corinthians 11:1
Follow my example, as I follow the example of Christ.

It is important to be a great student, and if I really try hard, I'll be perfect and I'll be just like Jesus. Sorry but, none of us can or ever will be like Jesus. That is IMPOSSIBLE, because Jesus was perfect. We are not and we will never be perfect. The goal is to try though. We need to do our best to live a Christ like life.

We are like an apprentice, and He is our Master Teacher!! We are learning from Him. Jesus has paved the road. It is our job to try our best to stay between the lines.

Is it important to be a great student? It is. And here's why; Hopefully you will share or already are sharing Jesus with others. Is there anyone you can think of right now, that you might want to tell about Jesus? Maybe you're in a small group. Maybe you've had a friend that you've helped through a tough time in the past. Maybe it's someone you see every day at school or work, but you haven't worked up the courage to talk to them yet. Even if you're not at this point, some day, someone may ask you about Him. Are you ready to tell someone else about Jesus?

How can I share Jesus with someone else?
Am I worried about what I will say?

_____

_____

_____

_____

_____

_____

_____

_____

_____

_____

_____

Luke 6:40
The student is not above the teacher, but everyone who is fully trained will be like their teacher.

What are the first steps in being a disciple?

Well the first step to discipleship is believing that Jesus Christ is our Savior and the Son of God. Have you accepted Jesus into your heart and understand that He died for your sins?

Now let's look at the 2nd half of v31–

"If you hold to my teaching" reveals the next step towards true discipleship. Following God's word is evidence of genuine faith.

The secret of eternal life is in His word. To be His disciple, we have to understand that He is our Lord and Savior.

The Truth—is another name for Jesus in the Bible. He is the Way, the Truth, and the Light...

John 4:16

If you study His word then you will know the Truth. The Truth does set you free from the bondage of sin.

Real disciples are both followers and learners. Are you ready to share Jesus with someone else? Will you be the student that pays close enough attention that you will be able to share all you know about Jesus?

Have I really accepted Jesus into my heart?

John 8: 31-32

To the Jews who had believed in Him, Jesus said, "If you hold to my teaching, you are really my disciples. Then you will know the truth, and the truth will set you free."

What do I use to guide me as a disciple? Let's see what Paul tells his student Timothy.

Use the Bible! The scriptures are God's authoritative word. God got the Bible started and inspired its writers. The Bible we have is the word God wants us to have. Here's the way I like to think about it, when I read it. It's like I'm sitting right there with Him telling me the story.

To be a disciple we have to understand His Word. For some it takes a lifetime. I am not an expert for sure, but that's ok. We just need to keep reading, keep studying, keep learning, and the most important part, start and keep sharing Him with others!!

Disciples are lifelong Learners, Teachers and Sharers. The only mission God ever gave us was... Make disciples.

Matthew 28: 18-20

Another aspect of being a disciple is living a life that can be an example for others. Are you living a life worth imitating? Eventually you will understand this perspective. You are actually always in discipleship mode!! Someone is always watching, so you're always teaching. Here is the example you can set. Learn all you can about The Word of God, then share with others what you know. Are you ready? I know you are! Then let's go!

What are some things I can use
to help me be a good disciple?
How has this week made me
think differently about discipleship?

2 Timothy 3: 16-17

All scripture is God-breathed and is useful for teaching, rebuking, correcting and training in righteousness, so that the servant of God may be thoroughly equipped for every good work.

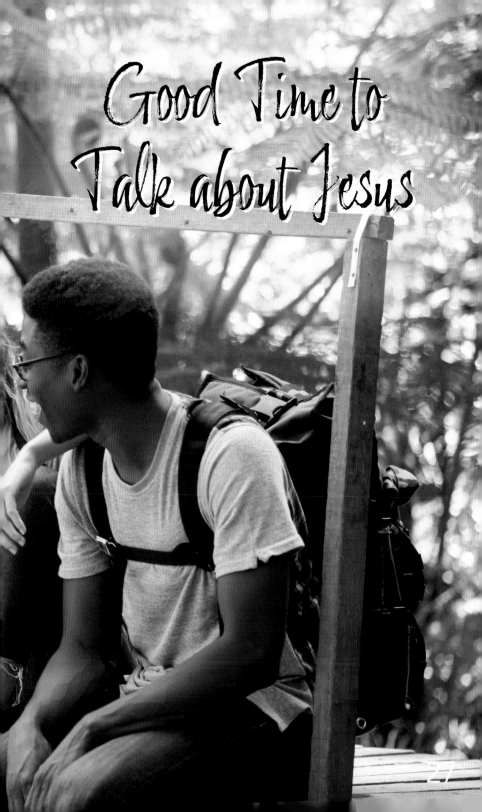

Good Time to
Talk about Jesus

Day 1

When is a good time to talk about Jesus? In the morning? At dinner? Before you go to bed? How about weekend family Bible study?

Can you believe a whole generation did not know God? So, either their parents did not do a very good job of introducing them to God. Or.... They were told about God but simply decided NOT to believe on their own.

The Israelite parents had failed to carry out an extremely important command God had given them:

Deuteronomy 6:6-7

These commandments that I give you today are to be on your hearts. Impress them on your children. Talk about them when you sit at home and when you walk along the road, when you lie down and when you get up.

You know, here's the deal! ANYTIME is a GREAT time to talk about Jesus. I'm not sure what will work best for you and hopefully your whole family, but one thing I can tell you is..... we need to start talking! We should spend some kind of time with Jesus EVERY day. I think that as we become rooted in Him on a daily basis, we will soon begin to have conversations organically. We need to NORMALIZE conversations about Jesus. 🙏❤📖

When is a good time to talk about Jesus?

Judges 2:10

After that whole generation had been gathered to their ancestors, another generation grew up who knew neither the Lord nor what he had done for Israel.

ANY TIME is a good time to talk about Jesus! But, the question is, will you be prepared for that conversation when it comes up? Let's review a verse that you saw last week.

God's word is "useful for teaching." So that verse really brings up two questions. Are you familiar with the Bible? And....do you want to share with others?

Listen, I'm not suggesting that you have to know the Bible from Genesis to Revelation. That takes YEARS of work!! I'm also not saying that Jesus should be the very first thing you talk about, when you meet someone, although that would be AWESOME!! But, after all, teaching may not even be one of your spiritual gifts.

What I am saying is that we need to be familiar with the word of God, continue to learn as we grow in relationship with Him, and then have the desire to share it with others.

When I read the bible, do I ever think about sharing things that I read with Someone else?

_____
_____
_____
_____
_____
_____
_____
_____
_____
_____

2 Timothy 3:14-17

But as for you, continue in what you have learned and have become convinced of, because you know those from who you learned it, and how from infancy you have known the Holy Scriptures, which are able to make you wise for salvation through faith in Christ Jesus. All scripture is God breaded and is useful for teaching, rebuking, correcting and training in righteousness, so that the servant of God may be thoroughly equipped for every good work.

Mark, I get what you're saying. I know we should share Jesus with others, but I don't think that I'm qualified to talk to someone about Jesus. I don't know what to say, and I don't want to sound foolish. I just get super nervous.

Ok, well I HOPE you do want to help others get to know Jesus. If you do, I think I can help you. Here's my advice for you. Don't worry so much about your qualifications, or sounding good, just focus on your willingness. 😊🧡🤎

He wants us to share Him with everyone...right? He's going to be with you! He's going to guide you! So... you're all set.

If you have accepted Jesus as your Savior, and have been saved, well then you know more than anyone who is not part of God's family. If Christ is in you, then live Christ like. If you are still nervous or unsure of yourself, think about it like this.... Simply allow God to speak to others through you. All you have to say is YES!!! READY... SET... YES!!

Do I really believe that my willingness is more important than feeling "qualified"?
Do I feel nervous when I think about sharing Jesus?

_____
_____
_____
_____
_____
_____
_____
_____
_____
_____
_____

Philippians 4:9

Whatever you have learned or received or heard from me, or seen in me—put it into practice. And the God of peace will be with you.

Let's look at it from this perspective. NOW is a good time to talk about Jesus, because that is exactly what He wants us to do!! It's as simple as that. Here's the deal..... being saved, receiving eternal life from our Father, means we "get to" bring others into our family. We should view this role as a privilege.

These seventy-two were chosen by Jesus to go out into small towns and villages and get them ready to receive Jesus. By this time in His ministry, time was of the essence. The time spent saving souls must be impactful. There was no time that could be wasted. Sending these disciples out in groups of two, means that 36 areas could be made ready at one time.

"The harvest is plentiful..."

There were literally thousands of people who wanted to have Jesus in their lives, but had no way of hearing the gospel. Picture Him talking to this group with a GREAT sense of URGENCY!! That URGENCY is just as great today as it was 2,000 years ago!! Time is critical! We simply cannot waste any more time! 🕐💜📖.

How will my willingness make a difference
in someone else's life?

_____
_____
_____
_____
_____
_____
_____
_____
_____
_____
_____

Luke 10:1-2

After this the Lord appointed seventy-two others and sent them out two by two ahead of him to every town and place where he was about to go. He told them, "The harvest is plentiful, but the workers are few. Ask the Lord of the harvest, therefore, to send out workers into his harvest field."

Hopefully y'all agree that NOW is a good time to talk about Jesus. I want you to understand that your willingness is more important than how much you know, because He will always be right beside us. Now, as we talk to others, we may face opposition and grow tired. Have you ever felt like you're the only one trying to walk with Jesus? It's ok to say that... Feeling that way is not any type of self righteousness. You may just simply be frustrated. It seems like you can't get anyone on the same page as you.

Paul is encouraging Timothy to be strong. It's so easy to get fired up about Jesus, and then lose momentum or become discouraged, because it seems like no one wants to walk with you.

You have to remain encouraged, knowing that at some point you will either be the perfect disciple to introduce someone to Jesus. Or, you will be the disciple that someone comes to and says, "Ok, tell me who Jesus is." You may be the reason that someone is saved.

THEN YOU will take on a role similar to Paul's, with Timothy. You will be someone's cheerleader, someone's rock, when they need strength. In every one of these instances you will receive your strength from the Holy Spirit. KEEP UP YOUR STRENGTH! KEEP UP YOUR COMMUNICATION THROUGH PRAYER! I too will pray for your strength!

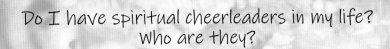

Do I have spiritual cheerleaders in my life?
Who are they?

_____
_____
_____
_____
_____
_____
_____
_____
_____
_____
_____

2 Timothy 2:1-2

You then, my son, be strong in the grace that is in Christ Jesus. And
the things you have heard me say in the presence of many witnesses
entrust to reliable people who will also be qualified to teach others.

What if? What if we continued to talk about Jesus. We are willing, we maintain our strength and our fire 🔥 for sharing the gospel story with people. Then those people continue in their new life of discipleship. What if the number of people who followed Jesus and shared the gospel became greater than the number of people who choose not to. Our world would be so much different! By the way, I think we can do it! Today's verse from Acts comes from a time when the disciples fought persecution, to continue their ministry.

Acts 5:17-41 shows the INCREDIBLE commitment of the disciples to their ministry. They were told to stop teaching by the leaders. The disciples informed them they would not stop. The disciples were thrown in jail, and an angel was sent to help them escape. They continued to teach, and were brought in again to appear before the high priest. They wanted to put them to death. But a Pharisee named Gamaliel stepped in with a more rational outlook.

In Acts 5:38-39

Therefore, in the present case I advise you: Leave these men alone! Let them go! For if their purpose or activity is of human origin, it will fail. But if it is from God, you will not be able to stop these men; you will only find yourselves fighting against God.

The disciples were physically beaten and then let go. They rejoiced in their suffering for Jesus. Think about the opposition they faced. They literally put their lives on the line to share the word of Jesus. Sure, we will face opposition today, but nothing like the disciples did 2,000 years ago. Thinking about that makes me want to share Jesus even more... for those who paved the way for me to be able to worship. 👐🙏

Am I willing to suffer to share Jesus?

Acts 6:7

So the word of God spread. The number of disciples in Jerusalem increased rapidly, and a large number of priests became obedient to the faith.

Today's reading is a great add to yesterday. It is a beautiful reminder from Paul. We have to continue to talk about Jesus even when we are faced with adversity.

Paul had no fear of continuing his ministry, spreading the gospel, even in the face of danger, including death. You see, Paul was not afraid to die. As you can see, he considers his life worth nothing. He does not care about the death of his earthly body. He knows he'll be in heaven with God, when he leaves his body. He died in Jesus on his journey to Damascus. He will remain committed to teaching the gospel until his earthly life is over. Paul certainly believed that ANY TIME and ANY PLACE was a good time to talk about Jesus. I agree with Paul 100%! Are you ready to start talking about Jesus?

What adversity could I be faced with?
How can I overcome it?

_____
_____
_____
_____
_____
_____
_____
_____
_____
_____
_____

Acts 20:22-24

And now, compelled by the Spirit, I am going to Jerusalem, not knowing what will happen to me there. I only know that in every city the Holy Spirit warns me that prison and hardships are facing me. However, I consider my life worth nothing to me; my only aim is to finish the race and complete the task the Lord Jesus has given me— the task of testifying to the good news of God's grace.

...not do any w[ork], ... nor thy servant, nor thy dau[ghter], ... nor thy cattle, nor thy ma[id] ... thy gate[s]: nor thy strang[er] ... 11 For in six days th[e] ... heaven and earth, the se[a], in them is, and rested the ... wherefore the LORD bles[sed] ... bath day, and hallowed it.

12 ¶ Honour thy father ... mother: that thy days ma[y] ... upon the land which the ... God giveth thee.

13 Thou shalt not kill.

14 Thou shalt not commi[t] ...

15 Thou shalt not ste[a]l.

16 Thou shalt not bear fal[se] ... against thy neighbour.

[1]7 Thou shalt not covet th[y] ... neighbour's house, thou shalt n[ot] ... [ne]ighbour's wife, nor h[is] ... [servan]t, nor his maidservant, ... [a]nd his ass, nor any thing ... [neighb]our's.

... all the people sa[w] ... of the lightnings, and ... [the] trumpet, and ... [sm]oking: and when th[ey] ... [i]t, they removed, and ...

... said unto ...

God's
Direction

43

There are many verses in the Bible about God's path for us. The path or the way to eternal life is so important for everyone in this world to find. How do you find that path, if you're not a Christian? Or....how do we stay on that path once we are on it? The answer is easy! We have to spend time in the word, which is our map to eternal life. So, this week, let's take a look at some of the verses that help us.

Ancient paths? Have you ever forgotten how to get somewhere? Here's the deal. There have been many times in my life where I've had to pull over and ask for directions. (before GPS)

So, I would roll down my window and ask someone for help. Now, that persons response was critical. There were two common scenarios:

1) Although the person was trying to help me, after like the fifth turn, I would tune them out and say thank you. I would pull away shaking my head saying "I'll just find the place myself." So I would do my own thing and not find my destination.

2) The other possibility is the similar. The person helping me, gives me perfect directions. But, I just wasn't listening quite good enough, and I end up making a bad turn and get lost again.

Think about how silly those two situations are. I admit to myself that I am lost. I take time to ask for help. And....then, I either don't listen closely enough, or decide not to listen at all.

Today's verse gives me the image of lost travelers looking for the right way to go but...They can't figure it out and.... They have chosen not to listen to anyone who does know the path to eternal life. So, they get caught up in a life of idolatry, thinking their way, is either just as good, or better.

Do I feel I am on a good path?
Am I on the path God has laid out for me?

That path to eternal life, as we read in scripture, is straight and narrow. Few people actually find it, and there are some people who don't care about finding it. Each one of us has access to that path, in the words of Jesus Christ. Once we find it we have to remember finding that path is not a one time event, it is a life long journey with Jesus. So, if you do have to pull over for directions, make sure you listen well! Listen with your whole heart!

Jeremiah 6:16

This is what the Lord says: Stand at the crossroads and look; ask for the ancient paths, ask where the good way is, and walk in it, and you will find rest for your souls. But you said, 'We will not walk in it'.

I love watching the sun rise early in the morning. I often spend that time out on the back patio, reading my devotional or working on other Bible reading. If I'm out there early enough, I actually have to turn the lights on, so I can see. But, as the sun comes up, I can turn them off again. If you think about it, our Christian journey is a lot like that.

That sun coming up in the morning reminds me of having the light of Jesus in our lives. When we have Him in our lives, we have His help when we are confronted by darkness, when we are tempted by Satan.

Now, here's the difference between the morning time on my back patio and our journey with Jesus......

When I go out on my patio early tomorrow morning, I'm going to have to turn the lights on again, until the sun comes up.

But....When we stay on the path of righteousness, we continue to have the light of Jesus inside of us, to light our journey, ALL the time! 🖤😊

AND.... In addition to that.... As we continue to spend time with Him and learn from Him, His light will become brighter and brighter. Soon, others will see the light of Jesus in us, and they will ask us about it. When they do, we can ask them to join us on our journey.

So, are you waiting for the sun to come up every day, so you have light? Or do you wake up with the light of Jesus glowing from you each and every day?

Am I waking up every day with the light of Jesus in my life?
Can everyone else around me see that?

Proverbs 4:18
The path of righteousness is like the morning sun, shining ever brighter till the full light of day.

Day 3

Have you ever gone hiking? Like in the mountains? If you have, I bet you probably did not go in your tennis shoes. Now, even if you are just a casual hiker, you probably have some kind of boots that you wear to hike in. Why not just wear tennis shoes?

Well, I would not wear tennis shoes for a number of reasons. Boots will give me more support than a tennis shoe, for the difficult landscape I may face.

Boots will give me better traction. Listen, losing your footing and falling in the mountains could result in a really long fall. 😳😓

So, the end result of me wearing boots for my hike is me getting to my destination, in one piece. 😊👢

Well, our Christian journey can be a lot like a hiking trip. We have to be prepared for some rough spots. There may be some holes or hazards that we don't even see until we get tripped up. That's where having a good pair of hiking boots will help us. We have to make sure we are prepared for our journey.

How can we be ready for our journey with Jesus? How can we stay on the right path? What is going to help us when we get tripped up, or come across an obstacle that we did not see coming? We need to prepare! That's the answer. We need to be in the word, EVERY DAY! Knowing The Word will help us keep our feet firmly planted on our path to eternal life! Did you ever think your Bible would be just like a pair of hiking boots! Let's get them laced up and ready to go.

God's Direction

How have I been tripped up on
my spiritual journey in the past?
How did I get back on the right track?

Psalm 17:5
My steps have held to your paths; my feet have not stumbled.

49

Wow! Today will be almost like a review of a few days we already looked at this week. Now even though we talked about having the right boots for that hike yesterday…. If we stay on the right path with Jesus, there's a good chance that our walk will be easier.

Let's go back and look at Sunday's text, "the ancient paths". So… those ancient paths to eternal life were traveled by others. Some people, of that time, just chose not to listen to them. So, here's the deal…. Surrounding ourselves with the RIGHT people, will also help us find the RIGHT path! AND then, we can help each other stay on track.

Now, don't be misled by the words used in today's verse. Look at it like this… the path to righteousness is NOT bumpy.   It is in fact smooth. But only if we stay on it. It is a narrow path, right? We see that in several Bible verses. It's when we think about going in a different direction, or when we get distracted and walk off the path, that we get lost or get caught in some sticker bushes. Yes, there may be some things we don't get to do, or shouldn't do, because those things are hazardous detours.

The right path is easier. I think that I feel it's easier, because it's the RIGHT WAY, even though it is narrow, because it is well lit by the words in our Bible!

So, my thoughts are… let's get with the right people and get on the right path! All those things we see in our peripheral vision… Ignore all that stuff! Keep your eyes focused on the lighted path in front of you. Follow Jesus.

Who do I have in my life that helps me stay on my path? Who can I help? Who can I share my boots with?

Isaiah 26:7

The path of righteousness is level; you, the Upright One, make the way of the righteous smooth.

Can anyone remember the two most important commands given to us by God? Hint: Jesus reminds us in the gospels.

Yes that's right! We find the answer in Matthew 22:37-40

Jesus replied: "Love the Lord your God with all your heart and with all your soul and with all your mind. This is the first and the greatest commandment. And the second is like it: Love your neighbor as yourself. All the Law and the Prophets hang on these two commandments."

So, let's get off the "path" today and look at the way to eternal life as more of a highway with lots of directional signs from God, kind of like big green ones that are all over the place now, that tell you where you are going. What would they all say?

- Love me, God
- Love your neighbor
- Love your parents
- Love your enemies
- Treat people fairly
- Treat people the way you would want to be treated

Now listen... there would not be any exit signs on the highway to eternal life—cause, well.....why would you want to get off of it, once you entered?

Love is the key to eternal life. It is simply the most important direction given to us in the old covenant and the great thing about love is that it is carried through to the new covenant with Jesus' ultimate sacrifice for you and I. The direction from God, to follow for today— LOVE HIM and show LOVE to ALL OTHERS. Not as simple as it sounds though, is it?

How good am I with following
directions toward my eternal life?
How good am I at giving directions to others?

Psalm 25:10
All the ways of the Lord are loving and faithful toward those who keep the commands of his covenant.

Have you ever done something where you had to follow directions.

- Cooking or baking?
- Playing a game?
- Putting something together?

If we don't follow directions, whatever it is that we are doing, will not turn out right.

There are three important directions / commands given in today's verses.

- Trust in the Lord
- Don't rely on just your own thoughts.
- Submit to Him

No matter what we are doing in life, hopefully we are ALL seeking God's will! That is in my prayers for each of you, and I pray for each of you to pray for that in your life. We should all submit ourselves to Him and trust that He will guide us where we need to be, and show us what He wants us to do.

If we change things up when baking cookies, well, they probably won't taste very good. If we don't read the directions on how to play a game, it will just be confusing. If we don't follow directions when putting something together, it's probably going to fall apart. What will our life look like if we don't follow God's direction?

What will my life look like if I choose not to follow God's directions?

_____
_____
_____
_____
_____
_____
_____
_____
_____

Proverbs 3:5-6

Trust in the Lord with all your heart and lean not on your own understanding; in all your ways submit to him, and he will make your paths straight.

Today is simple and beautiful. A verse we have all heard many, many times, but when I read it, it still gives me such peace.

Our Shepherd restores us. He refreshes us. He gives us new life and then shows us the right paths to take in life. He guides us forever, as long as we keep Him with us. If we want to get on the path to eternal life, we have to find Jesus. That is the ONLY way!

Following our own way will lead to our annihilation. I believe it will be a shame for any one of us who does not find Jesus Christ and accept Him as our Lord and Savior. The words on this are very clear in Revelation, at the end of Chapter 20. Please make sure you read the last few verses there.

So as we end the week on God's direction. I believe the choice is clear for everyone. Picture yourself at a fork in the road. One side is very welcoming. It is well lit, and seems to be level, with lots of signs letting us know which way we should go.

The other side has a sign that says, ENTER AT YOUR OWN RISK. The path is along a cliff and it is very dark and all of the signs say, YOU CAN DO WHATEVER YOU WANT.

↖ ↗
Acts 4:12   Revelation
John 5:24   20:11-15

which path will I choose?

_____
_____
_____
_____
_____
_____
_____
_____

We have to choose one path or the other. It's just that simple. I pray continuously for each of you to make the best choices possible, every day. I love you all.

Psalm 23:2-3

He makes me lie down in green pastures, he leads me beside quiet waters, he refreshes my soul. He guides me along the right paths for his names sake.

Listening

Hey everybody!! I need you to listen up!! ☺

Actually, I want you to listen for this whole next week, because listening is our theme. We all need to understand that listening is important in our own journey, but it's just as important to be a good listener as we disciple others. Let's go to 1 John to kick things off. John is reminding everyone to stay in God's word. Stay in the word, deny false teachers.

To remain in Christ, is to sustain a vital relationship with Him. Just like John wrote in his Gospel when he used the analogy of a branch that remains connected to the vine.

I'm telling you, our relationship with Him is VITAL. You either already have a great relationship with Jesus, or you may be walking toward one. That's your choice, your pace, your time. I will do anything you ever need me to do to help you, but I'm not going to be pushy about it. However, just like I expect you to be with me, I'm going to be honest with you. And YES... I believe our relationship with Jesus is VITAL. So...

Is this verse from today a warning? *...make sure what you've heard from the beginning, remains in you...* does this mean that our relationship with Christ can be lost?

You could honestly debate both sides of this argument... I've seen people or heard of people who have something happen in their life and they can't understand, or get "mad" at God, etc...

But, you have to listen to me, and REMEMBER, even if that happens... even if you get mad at HIM... He will NEVER leave you! Please don't EVER forget that. He loved you before you knew Him. He loves us no matter what!!!

Am I listening for God's word? Am I keeping His word with me?

_____

_____

_____

_____

_____

_____

_____

I will tell you this. I want to do everything in my power to talk to Him, read His word, and try to do what He would want me to do.   I think John gave us some amazing advice here. I'm going to listen! How about you?

1 John 2:24
As for you, see that what you have heard from the beginning remains in you. If it does, you will also remain in the son, and in the father.

Today we need to listen to James. He offers us some great advice in Chapter 1

That's my exclamation point! The Bible has a period. I want us all to be doers! That's really what James is talking about. James is emphasizing to them that their entire personality should be characterized by doing!

Professing Christians who are content with only hearing the Word are simply missing the most important part of the life of a Christian. Sharing the word and life of Jesus, which requires us to share our knowledge and our love. We have to "do" something with it. We have to pass it on, share with others, Inspire others, engage with others on their journey. True discipleship comes during the sharing process, the "doing" process. "Doing" life with others.

I wonder what James would say to us today? We may say we are Christians, but the real test is, do we believe what we "talk" about. Are we just saying and not doing? You see, we can profess a relationship with Jesus, but the real question is....Do we POSSES a relationship with Jesus?

Am I doing?
Am I sharing the story of Jesus with others?

_____

_____

_____

_____

_____

_____

_____

_____

_____

_____

James 1:22

Do not merely listen to the word, and so deceive yourselves. Do what it says!

So Paul is really talking about the oral communication of the Gospel that was going on, at that time.

Here is why listening is so important, for understanding. Faith doesn't come just from hearing the word of Jesus. Faith comes from what you understand. Faith comes from what you're willing to share as the truth and the light of Jesus. We cannot understand these things just by "hearing" something. We have to listen.

Paul is certainly telling everyone here that saving faith can only come about through the Gospel. Salvation is God's work alone.

This really shows us that there is no other way to be saved but by the explicit Gospel of Jesus Christ.

Look at Luke 11:28

He replied, "Blessed rather are those who hear the word of God and obey it."

Advice for the rest of your life...

Always listen with the intent for understanding... Your spouse, your friends, your boss, your employees, your coworkers, your parents, your children, etc... Will all appreciate it very much!!

When I "listen" to someone,
am I listening for understanding?
When I read God's word,
am I listening for understanding?

Romans 10:17

Consequently, faith comes from hearing the message, and the message is heard through the word about Christ.

Please listen to me?!?! Just follow my instructions! We've all heard this before, somewhere in our lives, probably at school or work.

Well, I have a great lead in to today, a year ago we went on a white water rafting trip. Before we could go, we had to show up an hour early so we could "LISTEN" to a guide give us instructions. For what reason??? TO KEEP US SAFE!! I tried to call ahead and get the 45 minute tutorial out of the way early, but they would not let me. "Sir, this is the way we operate! You have to follow OUR instructions, or you cannot go on OUR trip. Now, if you have any other questions, you will be able to speak to the guide, when you get here." CLICK!!

Well, this made me start to think. No... not about canceling my trip. ☺ But about the fact that the young lady on the phone was just listening to her boss and following her instructions. I started to think about it like this:

God is our LIFE GUIDE! We can talk to Him any time we want, right?!?!

Let's go way back today to Exodus, and listen to Moses and God. In chapter 15, Moses was leading Israel through the desert of Shur. They could not drink the water, because it was bitter. The Lord showed Moses a piece of wood, Moses threw it in the water, and it became fit to drink. Then The Lord spoke through Moses... Wow!! We could break this verse into 2 days?!?! But I won't!

The problem with so many people is that we do not diligently listen to the voice of the Lord. We have a terrible habit of doing what is right in our sight, not what is right in God's sight.

The most important part of this verse... "I am the Lord, who heals you."

When someone is trying to share something important with me, do I really listen to what they have to say, or am I just kind of waiting for them to get finished?

_____

_____

_____

We must listen to The Lord and walk in His ways... if we want His blessings. God was trying to get Israel to a point of faith and trust that would be acceptable to Him. They failed test after test, because they just wouldn't listen! They complained at every problem, instead of believing. We will see them wander in the wilderness 40 years on a trip that should have taken a few days, because they just didn't listen and had such a lack of faith.

How often do we just wander in our lives today, when we should be LISTENING to our Life Guide Jesus Christ? We have access to Him and the "safety manual" any time we want it or need it. Have you looked at your manual today? Have you talked to our Guide? Are you listening to what He says?

Exodus 15:26

He said, "If you listen carefully to the Lord your God and do what is right in His eyes, if you pay attention to his commands and keep all his decrees, I will not bring on you any of the diseases I brought on the Egyptians, for I am The Lord, who heals you."

Communication (LISTENING) is a two way street! Right? Has God ever answered prayers for you? He certainly has for me! Well, for Him to answer my prayer, He has to hear me.

What is God's promise to us? Seek and you shall find, knock and the door will be opened for you.

What a wonderful feeling that is, to know that God has heard my individual prayer. Of all the millions of people in this world, God hears me!! And He answers me!

"He delivered me from all my fears."

Having fear is having a lack of faith in God. God will help us with all of our fears. It can be a fear of something, or a fear of a specific time in your life. He is ALWAYS there for us!

Put your fears in God's hands. Call out to Him! He's a GREAT LISTENER. The question is, are we listening with our whole heart, or are we only listening for what we WANT Him to say? Here's the deal...It's going to be difficult for us to hear Him, if we've already decided what we want Him to say.

How much time do I spend in prayer?
Am I really listening to God's response
to my prayers?

Psalm 34:4
I sought the Lord, and He answered me; He delivered me from all
my fears.

Back to the Old Testament again today.

There will be times in your life, that you will "tune" someone out. You won't listen. How can I be so sure? I've been the tuner outer... 😂 ...that's why. And, I will admit that I have tuned Jesus out, and didn't listen to Him. You see, there are too many times we don't listen. We are convinced we know what's best!

We DO NOT know better than Jesus. We have to pay attention. But the key question is, are we listening with our ears and our hearts. You see, we hear with our ears, BUT... understanding comes from our heart. Our heart creates what I call a commitment to listening. Once you understand that, your life will change.

Here's the deal today! Short and sweet!! Listen to Him. Stay true to Him. Hold Him close to your heart. Most importantly, talk to Him, and listen to what He tells you.

Have there been times in my life
that I have tuned Jesus out?

_____

_____

_____

_____

_____

_____

_____

_____

_____

_____

_____

Proverbs 4:20-22

My son, pay attention to what I say; turn your ear to my words. Do not let them out of your sight, keep them within your heart; for they are life to those who find them and health to ones whole body.

Let's listen to Jesus on our last day of listening!!

You see, we can hear the word! We can listen to Him! But, we have to put what we hear into action! We can go to church EVERY Sunday! We can go to youth Every Sunday! But it does us no good, until we start applying the things we learn to our own lives.

Compare the house to our lives. Our rock that we must build our lives on is Jesus Christ. We all have great days and tough days in our lives. The difference in the life of a Christian is that we face problems differently. A wise person seeks the answers to life's problems in our instruction manual (The Bible). We pray and ask God to help us through our problems. They do not overwhelm us, because our strength is not just coming from us. Our strength is also in Jesus. We turn to Him for help and he talks to us, and gets us through anything!! All we have to do, is listen!! He loves us so so much!!

Thank you for a great week of listening.

When I have a problem, do I turn to Jesus? How? This week, what have I learned about how I listen?

Matthew 7:24-25

Therefore everyone who hears these words of mine and puts them into practice is like a wise man who built his house on the rock. The rain came down, the streams rose, and the winds blew and beat against that house; yet it did not fall, because it had its foundation on the rock.

Heart

Day 1

We can all learn something from our past experiences, right? In some of the weeks leading up to this one, I referred to making more room in our heart for Jesus, by possibly getting rid of some other things that take up our time. In today's verse Joshua is referring to the heart as us understanding and knowing that all of God's promises are true.

This was Joshua's farewell to the leaders of Israel. (v1-3) At the end of v3 he emphasizes to the people, "It was the Lord your God who fought for you."

Here is the teachable moment for us, from these verses. He has never given us a reason to doubt. He will always be there for us! God expects / wants all of our heart! He wants everything we have, because He gives us everything He has!! He gave us Jesus, who gave Himself up for us.

I want you to understand, to walk with Jesus, we have to be all in. And…. Also understand that along the way, there may be times, where you actually question your faith. I promise that is ok. It is just a time to get re focused. Just so you know that you're not alone, let me share something with you …. I love Jesus with all my heart. But yesterday, I didn't spend any time with Him. I got busy. My day got away from me. I felt terrible. So, you see, even when we feel we have the strongest of commitments, we can still fall short. Guess what? God still loves me as much as He did yesterday.

Have I made room in my heart for Jesus?

Joshua 23:14

Now I am about to go the way of all the earth. You know with all your heart and soul that not one of all the good promises the Lord your God gave you has failed. Every promise has been fulfilled; not one has failed.

We've seen a lot of scripture and talked often about loving God with ALL our heart. We've discussed getting to go through a transformation. What does that really look like?

So, we get to have our hearts changed. Obviously, at that moment, there is a trust we have in Him. That trust, over time, becomes more and more amazing. We can begin to let go of things that have weighed us down forever, because we can take those burdens to Him.

(Psalm 55:22)

Here is how I look at v4.

Fifteen minutes with Jesus, right? At first, maybe we have to make "on purpose" time, to spend with Him. We may have to put other things aside, and say ok, this is my Jesus time! Over time, I'm hoping your time spent with Him becomes the priority. 😊 💜 Then you may even be able to help a friend spend more time with Him Also.

As we intentionally enjoy the time we spend with Jesus, in the Bible, at youth events, in prayer, etc... then He is actually going to change our wishes, to the point where we understand what He wants for us. At that point He is pleased to grant us our desires. As we truly engage our hearts in Jesus, He will show us what is best! He will show us His will for our lives.

Do I take my burdens to Jesus?
Do I trust Him with everything?

Psalm 37:3-4

Trust in the Lord and do good; dwell in the land and enjoy safe pasture. Take delight in the Lord, and He will give you the desires of your heart.

Will having Jesus in my heart make me a healthier person?

Most definitely the answer to that is YES!

On some level, Whether we are a Christian or not, we've all experienced that our mood can have an impact on our physical health. When we have a great day, a good test grade, when we win the big game, when we get good news, there's just a little extra bounce in our step. Right? As Christians, our joy is like part of our inheritance. A deep trust in God, with all our heart, becomes good medicine. It is a proven fact that people who think good thoughts feel better! If we truly have Jesus in our hearts, our joy can light up any room we walk into.

On the other hand negative thoughts can consume us, make us feel miserable, and actually contribute to poor health. Think about those tougher days; head down, kicking the stone across the parking lot…. Those days kinda stink.

My bad days did not go away, when I became a Christian. Wait, what? No… I still have bad days. But the bad days are fewer than what I used to have, because of the focus I put on Jesus. I just feel so much better.

Now, let me be clear; I am NOT saying that believers are healthier than non-believers. I am NOT saying that believers will live longer than non-believers. What I am saying is that being in Jesus with all our heart will make us beam with joy! I really like that option. How bout we light up the world together!!

When I spend time with Jesus,
how does it make me feel?

Proverbs 17:22
A cheerful heart is good medicine, but a crushed spirit dries up the
bones.

These people are really starting to listen to this guy. We have to stop Him. Let's try to trick Him. Let's trip Him up. All of our laws are so important. They are too important for this Jesus to be messing everything up.

You have to understand, the "expert in the law" would have been a VERY respected teacher of Old Testament Law. "Testing Him" implies that he was trying to draw Jesus into an argument regarding the Pharisees' extensive interpretation of over 600 laws. Jesus was not going to get into an argument. He simply replied that we have to love God... with everything we have. Our responsibility is to make God #1 in our life! Deuteronomy 6:5

There is a very good reason why this is most important. If we can truly give all our love to God, and stay focused on Him, the desires of our heart will become His will for us. It will make it so much easier for us to follow all His other instructions, about everything else, because pleasing Him will become what's most important to us. Growing closer to Him in our relationship, our focus will change. We will gain better understanding of His will. We will begin to see what He wants us to do.

Do I love God more than everything else in my life?

Matthew 22: 34-38

Hearing that Jesus had silenced the Sadducees, the Pharisees got together. One of them, an expert in the law, tested Him with this question: "Teacher, which is the greatest commandment in the law?" Jesus replied: "Love the Lord your God with all your heart and with all your soul and with all your mind. This is the first and greatest commandment."

God is not hiding from us. In today's verse Jeremiah is speaking the words of God to those in exile. v10 *This is what the Lord says...*

In the following few verses, He's assuring them that He has a plan for them to prosper and have a future.

He makes sure they understand, none of this will happen until you seek Me with all of your heart. God wants their heart. He wants our heart. But, just as we do today, they had to believe in their hearts that God existed, before they would seek Him.

All your heart does not mean you have to be perfect, but it does mean you have to seek Him with sincerity! God doesn't expect us to be perfect, but He does want us to be present. You have to mean it! It can't be just because someone told you to, or because you are supposed to. It has to be because you sincerely want to find God and have Him in your heart.

Trust me, He wants us to find Him. He's not hiding from us. To be saved, we have to have our heart focused on God! Romans 10: 9-10

Just as we are promised in Matthew 7:7 "Ask and it will be given to you; seek and you will find; knock and the door will be opened for you."

All we have to do is seek Him. Run to Him. God is not hard to find! This is not a game of hide and seek. He's waiting for us with open arms.

Am I present in my life with Jesus?
Do I understand that He loves me unconditionally?

Jeremiah 29:13
You will seek me and find me when you seek me with all your heart.

Remember that "thing" you had when you were a little kid, that always made everything better? What was it?

- blanket
- stuffed animal
- toy

Do you still have it? Are you going to keep it?

Think about having God in your heart. How valuable is the guidance we receive from Him? Isn't that a comforting feeling? Doesn't talking to Him make you feel better? In today's verses the Psalmist is referring to God's statutes.

So, once we have God in our heart, then we have to understand how important it is to keep Him there. God's teachings are the greatest thing we are ever going to have. We need to treat them as our most valued possession. We also need to make sure we pass those teachings on. Treat them like an inheritance, that we get to hand over to someone else.

We have so many types of family traditions today. I would like all of us to make passing God's teachings on to everyone, our family group tradition. We have to ask ourselves, is God's word the joy of my heart? Are we going to keep His word in our heart forever?

What is that "thing" or "place" in my life
that gives me a secure feeling?
Do I feel security from Jesus?

Psalm 119: 111-112
Your statutes are my heritage forever; they are the joy of my heart.
My heart is set on keeping your decrees to the very end.

Forever and ever!

There really is nothing more important in our life than loving God, and trusting Him!

In fact, it's a matter of life and death. It is mission critical.

...write them on the tablet of your heart ...keep it in your life forever! Think about it like this. I did this a few years ago... get out a piece of paper and a pen. Think about 10 ways that you can show your love and trust to God. Ten things you can really focus on and commit to. Now, go ahead and write them down, write them on the notes page ☞☞☞ Think of it as writing them on the "tablet of your heart!"

Put them somewhere that you will see them frequently as a reminder.

You may want to change them up... every few months... or yearly... or keep them the same forever. The idea is that it is one more way to keep God in our heart.

We all work on our relationships with the people in our lives, right? Well, we all need to work on our relationship with God, too. Having Him, and keeping Him in our heart FOREVER is not only the most important relationship we will EVER have, it is also the most rewarding relationship we will ever have!

What are 10 things I can do
to show my love and trust to God?

Proverbs 3: 3-4

Let love and faithfulness never leave you; bind them around your neck, write them on the tablet of your heart. Then you will win favor and a good name in the sight of God and man.

Truth

Do you know what is true, all the time?

How do you know what the truth is? Let's face it. We live in a world where the truth can be difficult to see or understand some times. I mean, we have our own thoughts on everything, right? Then, we may have friends who are pulling us in a different direction, and then social media is telling us something entirely different. We all have our own thoughts and feelings. EVERYONE has an opinion on EVERYTHING! Right? Where is the truth in all of it? Hopefully, The TRUTH is in us.... Somewhere!!!

It's kind of like true north vs magnetic north. True North is a FIXED point on the earths axis. Magnetic North is the direction that a compass needle points to, aligning with the earths magnetic field.

So.... Here's what's interesting.... The magnetic north SHIFTS, it changes over time, as the earths magnetic core changes. It is NOT a fixed point.

Jesus is THE TRUE NORTH in our spiritual life! He NEVER changes. He remains TRUE! We know where to find Him, and we know that He's going to lead us in the right direction. Jesus WAS, Jesus IS, and Jesus WILL BE...

Crazy fact.... The difference between true north and magnetic north on the globe can be as much as 300 miles (!!) depending where you're at....

How do I determine what the
truth is in my life today?

_____
_____
_____
_____
_____
_____
_____

So, follow Jesus, and His word and end up EXACTLY where you're supposed to be. Follow anything or anyone else and end up…, well??? Who knows where? I'm going with the sure thing! I'm following Jesus! How about You?

John 1:14
The Word became flesh and made his dwelling among us. We have seen his glory, the glory of the one and only son, who came from the Father, full of grace and truth.

Do you want to know the Truth? Do you want me to tell you about the Truth? Yes?   Well, good! Because we already share the Truth in this text! Let's look at what the Apostle John wrote is his letter to a group of churches in Ephesus.

John was writing to encourage and strengthen this group of believers faith. Take notice how he starts this verse, at the end of this letter. "We know"—this serves as an assurance to them, as it does to us today. We know who Jesus is. He is the Son of God. As Christians we've accepted this to be TRUE! We believe in The Truth and want to share Him with others!

Two important things to understand as truth from today. First, God has given us Jesus! Second, because we have Jesus in our lives, we gain truth in understanding what our spiritual life should look like, and what we "get" because of it!

In the last verse, he's closing the letter, almost with like one last quick thought that he remembered to remind us of. Please remember to stay away from idols. Two points here—distance yourselves from false teachers, and keep Jesus #1 in your heart.   That's the TRUTH!!

Is Jesus in the #1 slot in my heart?
Are there idols that are taking up time
I could be spending with Him?

_____

_____

_____

_____

_____

_____

_____

_____

1 John 5:20-21

We know also that the Son of God has come and has given us understanding, so that we may know him who is true. And we are in him who is true by being in his Son Jesus Christ. He is the true God and eternal life. Dear children, keep yourselves from idols.

Jesus told the truth! Ok, I know, I know, you already know that ♥😊📱
Let's take a look at Jesus talking to the disciples today.

What a beautiful reminder of what He was sending the disciples—
The Holy Spirit—Although He was going to leave them physically, He
was still going to leave them with His Spirit. They would NEVER be
alone.

My last sentence in the first paragraph.... I didn't only mean today as
in this text......I meant today, as in this point in time. Reread today's
verse as if Jesus is speaking directly to you. Why? Because He is!
He's talking directly to you, and me, from 2,000 years ago.

We also, MUST testify about the Truth! You ready? How will you tell
someone about Jesus? What will you say? Keep in mind that you may
be testifying about Jesus to a new believer, or to someone who already
knows Him, but may need your encouragement.

When I read today's verse as if Jesus is speaking directly to me, how does that make me feel?

_____
_____
_____
_____
_____
_____
_____
_____
_____
_____
_____

John 15:26-27

When the Advocate comes, whom I will send to you from the Father—the Spirit of truth who goes out from the Father—he will testify about me. And you also must testify, for you have been with me from the beginning.

Do you tell the truth? Can you tell the truth?

Sometimes we struggle with it, right? Most of us, I'm sure, have embellished a story at some time, adding our own little, extra part to the story.

I love Proverbs, short and to the point. Solomon reminds us here of God's distaste toward people who don't tell the truth, but then immediately makes sure we know that God loves the truth!

If you have not thought about it before, the truth is so important to God, that He told us so in one of His commands.

—*You must not give false testimony against your neighbor*—

The fact that He told us in the Ten Commandments really heightens the importance for me!

Have you ever heard someone, describe someone else as…. "He's a man of his word."

When someone uses that phrase, they are telling whoever is listening that this person in trustworthy. They speak the truth. Well, as Christians, we should speak the truth.   Our word is our bond. We should all be a person of our word, just as Jesus is.

Are there times in my life
that I try to keep the truth from God?
Would other people consider me
a person of my word?

_____

_____

_____

_____

_____

_____

_____

_____

_____

_____

Proverbs 12:22
The Lord detests lying lips, but he delights in people who are trustworthy.

We need to know the Truth, so we can know and share the truth. And NOT get caught up in what isn't true or simply doesn't matter.

Ok, the Bible is BIG! There's A LOT of information in there! And... there are many, many, parts of scripture that people debate about, all the time. People who are much smarter than I am. 😂💜

Those debates can be time wasters and take us away from what we should really be focused on, which is spreading the gospel message. In today's verses Paul is instructing Timothy about false teachers but also warning him to avoid these pointless conversations.

Recently, a friend and I were discussing scripture and we did NOT agree. I wanted to PROVE I was right, and then he made a great point. The only winner in the debate was Satan, because it was pulling us away from what we should be focused on. He's sneaky like that.

So, what is the truth? Well, there are A LOT of things in the Bible which are easy truths to understand and are important to us in sharing the message. There are 4 truths that I think all of us can focus on and share with ease...

- God created everything. He created us. We belong to Him
- God loves us. He gave us free will. Because of that we sin. That sin separates us from Him.
- Jesus is the Son of God. God gave Him to us to show us a perfect life and to be in relationship with Him. Then, He died for our sins. His sacrifice was for our eternal life. His life for ours.
- Although He died for us, that's not all there is to it. We have to believe in Jesus and accept Him with our whole heart. We have been invited into His family. All we have to do is say yes. That's the truth! You in?

What are the truths in the Bible
that I can share with others?

_____

_____

_____

_____

_____

_____

_____

_____

_____

_____

2 Timothy 2:15-16

Do your best to present yourself to God as one approved, a worker who does not need to be ashamed and who correctly handles the word of truth. Avoid godless chatter, because those who indulge in it will become more and more ungodly.

Day 6

Where can we find the truth? Well, we shouldn't have to go too far to find it. Hopefully the truth is in our hearts. You may have heard today's verses before. Jesus is talking to the Samaritan woman, at the well.

A few verses before today's verse, the woman is trying to remove Jesus' focus from her, by asking Him to settle an argument. The question of where worship should take place, on the mountain, or in the temple?

Jesus showed great focus, as only He can. He informed her quickly that true worship has nothing to do with where it happens in a geographical sense. True worship is determined by what is in our hearts. As true worshipers, we have the power of the Holy Spirit in our hearts. So, it doesn't matter where we worship at. It doesn't matter if it is in a church, someone's house, or my back patio. What does matter is what is the location of Jesus in our life? Is He in our hearts?

What is the location of Jesus in my life?
Do I have the Truth in my heart?

John 4:23-24

Yet a time is coming and has now come when the true worshipers will worship the Father in the spirit and in truth, for they are the kind of worshipers the Father seeks. God is spirit, and his worshipers must worship in the Spirit and in truth.

Have you ever heard the saying, You can't judge a book by its cover.

There will be times where it appears that people may speak the truth, but they are actually false teachers.

In case you haven't noticed. There is a lot of content in the Bible that gets debated. People have different views and their own interpretations. Some thoughts are interesting and some just take our time away from Jesus. I have two important points I want you to remember.

- People may not like something that Jesus said, and that's their choice. But…. They can't say that Jesus never said it.
- Any time, any two people end up in a debate or even an argument over scripture, Satan wins. That's what he wants. He wants to keep us away from what's most important. Jesus!!!

The anointing we have as believers is the Holy Spirit that we have in us. Teaching from other people is important for our spiritual growth. The Spirit we have will help us understand the difference between right and wrong. The Spirit will guide us in truth!

When I do struggle understanding something in the Bible, who do I go to for help?

1 John 2:26-27

I am writing these things to you about those who are trying to lead you astray. As for you, the anointing you received from him remains in you, and you do not need anyone to teach you. But as his anointing teaches you about all things and as that anointing is real, not counterfeit—just as it has taught you, remain in him.

Yes, I believe in Jesus. Does that mean I'm saved? I think there is a lot more to our salvation than simply saying yes to Jesus. It is a great start though. Some of us may have questions / conflicts about becoming a Christian. For example, do I really have to deny myself and lose my life? What's that all about?

In v35 Jesus asks them an interesting question about spirituality. For me it comes down to this. Do you want to live a life that the world is accepting of? Or, do you want to give up some of the sinful things in your life and live your life following Jesus? We simply cannot have both... our sinful flesh MUST die for us to live with Jesus.

What are we REALLY giving up so we can live our life with Jesus? We certainly are not making anywhere near the sacrifice He made for us. When I look at it like that, it's honestly a pretty simple decision. I choose to try to live my life in a way that Jesus will be accepting of. Now, if the rest of the world accepts me, knowing that Jesus is my BEST FRIEND, that's AWESOME!! Let's get together and worship. If they don't accept me because of that, their loss!! But everyone in the world needs to understand... the greatest mistake we can make in life is not knowing Jesus!

What things can I give up in my life to spend more time with Jesus?

_____

_____

_____

_____

_____

_____

_____

_____

_____

_____

Mark 8:34-35

Then He called the crowd to Him along with His disciples and said: "Whoever wants to be my disciple must deny themselves and take up their cross and follow me. For whoever wants to save their life will lose it, but whoever loses their life for me and for the gospel will save it."

My salvation makes me feel so safe. As I walk with Jesus, it feels like I have this AMAZING, immovable force with me... everywhere I go!!

I mean... how safe do those two verses make you feel? The emotions I feel, when I think of Jesus being my ROCK, my foundation, just give me this sense of devotion back to Him, that may even be hard for some people to understand. How does He resemble being a rock in our lives? Well, He's NOT budging! He wants us! He's not going anywhere! He is patiently waiting for us to come to Him, and spend time with Him.

Our salvation will give us so much strength and confidence. But we can only have that when we truly trust in Him and completely turn our lives over to Him. He's a strong presence in our lives, once we get to know Him. He is our protector. And what's truly amazing is that He wants that relationship with each and everyone of us. He loves us all the same, and He promises us a life with Him forever. Knowing that we have that promise from Him... doesn't that make you feel safe also?

How safe do I feel knowing I have Jesus in my life?

_____

_____

_____

_____

_____

_____

_____

_____

_____

_____

_____

Psalm 62:1-2

Truly my soul finds rest in God; my salvation comes from Him. Truly He is my rock and my salvation; He is my fortress, I will never be shaken.

One of my favorite things to think about, when thinking about Jesus, is all of the different names that He is called by in the Bible. My favorite is Shepherd. In fact that is how I pray to Him.

v7. Jesus tells us, that He is the gate. He is our Shepherd.

v8. He is referring to the many false teachers who had come before Him.

v9. Our only way to salvation is through Him. Believing in Him and having a relationship with Him.

v10. This thief is the devil. His mission is to seek and destroy.

A shepherd represents protection for their sheep. A shepherd loves their sheep and cares for them. A shepherd guides their sheep to green grass. Their sheep belong to them, they are responsible for them.

Jesus does all of that for us. He loves us! He's going to protect us! He's going to guide us! He tells us "He has come so that we may have life." Jesus, The Greatest Shepherd of all time showed us His love and Power of His commitment to us, by laying down His life for us, His sheep, on the cross. Our Shepherd gives us our salvation!

How has Jesus shown His love for me?

John 10:7-10

Therefore Jesus said again, "Very truly I tell you, I am the gate for the sheep. All who have come before me are thieves and robbers, but the sheep have not listened to them. I am the gate; whoever enters through me will be saved. They will come in and go out, and find pasture. The thief comes only to steal and kill and destroy; I have come that they may have life, and have it to the full."

The Gate continued:

Gosh, this road to salvation is tight. I keep on hitting the rumble strips. It's hard to keep it between the ditches some times. Why is this path so small?

Jesus made it clear, on many occasions, that following Him would not be easy. Following Him calls for us to submit to Him, confess things to Him, and ask for forgiveness. It requires us to gain knowledge and seek the truth! Then, once we have an understanding of the truth, we have to be willing to obey His word.

NEWS FLASH!!!!!!!

Let's be honest with each other, we ALL sin. It's easy to sin right? Just think about all of the sinful things we have in our world tempting us. We have to work hard! We have to keep both hands on the wheel. Jesus doesn't want a halfhearted effort from us!! He wants our best. He wants us to have our eyes on Him, and our heart in Him constantly!

So YES, the gate to an eternal life with Him is narrow! Like the end of today's verse says... only a few find it! That's why it's so important to spend time with Him EVERY day! The more we stay focused on Him, the stronger we'll become. So, don't let that narrow gate intimidate you; focus on the journey and what's waiting for you!

Do I share EVERYTHING in my life with Jesus?
What am I holding back from Him?

_____

_____

_____

_____

_____

_____

_____

_____

_____

_____

Matthew 7:13-14

Enter through the narrow gate. For wide is the gate and broad is the road that leads to destruction, and many enter through it. But small is the gate and narrow the road that leads to life, and only a few find it.

As Christians, are we waiting for Heaven?

Have you ever heard someone say, "This is Heaven on earth."

Can we have Heaven on earth? What does that phrase even mean?

Most times people will say something like that, when they are in a very peaceful place, like a favorite vacation spot.

In Matthew 6:9-13 Jesus taught us how to pray... *Your Kingdom come, Your will be done, on earth as it is in Heaven...*

Bring salvation to those who are waiting for Him? Heaven is and will be AMAZING! Here is my thought for today—Why wait for Heaven? Why don't we live that life now. It's so clear in the Lord's Prayer that Jesus is calling us to bring heaven to earth. So, LET'S DO IT!! 🤍👍

It tells us in the Bible that on judgment day, Jesus will appear to those who are looking for Him. Philippians 3:20

We have one earthly life to live, right? Why not live it EVERY DAY, with Jesus in it. Let's start sharing our eternity with Him right now. And while doing that, also sharing Him with EVERYONE else!

Where is my peaceful place, my Heaven on earth?
Am I waiting for Heaven,
or am I trying to live that life now?

_____
_____
_____
_____
_____
_____
_____
_____
_____
_____

Hebrews 9:28

So Christ was sacrificed once to take away the sins of many; and He will appear a second time, not to bear sin, but to bring salvation to those who are waiting for Him.

Our salvation comes from our faith... our belief in Jesus Christ. To strengthen our faith, we have to use it. There may be times that will require that strength for us to share Jesus with others. In today's reading Paul tells us that he is not ashamed of the gospel.

Why did Paul stress that he was not ashamed of the gospel? Well, he faced some pretty terrible opposition. Look at his life... he was run out of several cities. He was made fun of. He was stoned. He was beaten... several times. He was even thrown in prison in Philippi. Still, he remained hungry to share the gospel in Rome. Even after all the intimidating opposition he received, Paul remained fearless in his quest of sharing the gospel with anyone who would listen.

Today, we don't face quite the same kind of opposition Paul did, not even close. But, there will be times when it won't be easy. How bold are you willing to be to express your joy of the shepherd who's saved us?!

What opposition will I face, if I try to share the gospel with someone?
What can I do to overcome that opposition?

_____
_____
_____
_____
_____
_____
_____
_____
_____

Romans 1:16-17

For I am not ashamed of the gospel, because it is the power of God that brings salvation to everyone who believes; first to the Jew, then to the Gentile. For in the gospel the righteousness of God is revealed—a righteousness that is by faith from first to last, just as it is written: "The righteous will live by faith."

Do we need reminders? Do we need reassurance?

Jesus is always with us. He reminds us of His eternal presence in our lives in today's verse.

We know Jesus is committed to us. What I want you to think about as we finish up our salvation theme is... how committed are you to Him? There are lots of people who believe in God and believe Jesus is our Savior. And yes, we can go to church, read the Bible, and even go through confirmation, catechism, or what ever it is that your church denomination calls it. But, that's not enough. We need to understand that what Jesus expects from us, cannot end with our conversion. Our conversion is just the beginning.

Our belief in Jesus, our salvation, comes with the requirement of sharing Him with others. Jesus not only told us to preach but told us what to preach. And He showed us how. His promise to be with us always ensures our success in spreading His word. But, we have to be willing to do it. Hopefully we all understand that... salvation is not just a one time event in our life... it is a DAILY path we must travel. "Our" salvation requires OUR participation! Are you committed to a relationship with Jesus? He already told us, He'll be with us always. If He was sitting next to you right now, would you make the same commitment to Him?

How committed am I to a relationship with Jesus?
How committed am I to sharing Him with others?

Matthew 28:20
And teaching them to obey everything I have commanded you. And surely I am with you always, to the very end of the age.

Trust

Don't worry, I got this! Trust me!!

Trust is a huge thing for us. It is part of our friendships and it is part of our relationship with God. Let's start this week in Matthew.

Jesus is telling us a lot here in Matthew 6... As you look at the verses, ask yourself this question. Is Jesus giving us a command, not to worry? The answer is that it's not so much a command as it is an invitation to rest in the arms of our Heavenly Father.

"We" tend to freak out a lot. We worry about this, we're scared of that... Grades, friends, what someone else said, etc...

Sometimes we get way out of whack, when all we need is a little trust. There are a lot of great stories about trust in the Bible. A lot of them have a common theme.

So many times in our lives it's all about... me, me, me. When it should be about Jesus, Jesus, Jesus.

Think about all the things in your life that cause you to worry. The next time one of those things creeps into your mind and is about to put you in a dull mood... or even ruin your day... picture Jesus holding out His hand and asking you to trust Him. All you have to do is grab His hand. He will guide you through.

Remember it's an invitation to trust in him, not a law to obey. We all have people in our lives that we trust, right? We may just need to put Jesus in that #1 slot!!!

Who do I really trust in my life?
Do I trust Jesus?

Matthew 6:25-26

Therefore I tell you, do not worry about your life, what you will eat
or drink; or about your body, what you will wear. Is not life more
than food, and the body more than clothes? Look at the birds of the
air; they do not sow or reap or store away in barns, and yet your
Heavenly Father feeds them. Are you not much more valuable than
they?

Trust yourself? Common sense?

I've got EVERYTHING under control. I don't need anyone's help. Have you ever said something like that. I know I have. I mean, it's just easier, right? First of all, we don't always want everyone knowing what's going on in our lives, because it's just none of their business.... Or.... If it's my situation, my problem... well then it's gotta be my solution, right? What about Jesus? Are you willing to trust Him?

First part of Proverb's 3, verse 5–

All your heart. Not half, not some of... All

Second part of v5

Don't rely on just yourself. He is there to guide us, help us!

I believe spending time, some way, on a regular basis, with Him keeps us grounded in common sense. His wisdom is filled with common sense. We need to trust his word. Here's the deal, there isn't anything that we can take to Him that is going to take Him by surprise. He knows what you're struggling with. Just tell Him! Turn it over to Him! Ask Him to show you His will!

His love is so great for us! Let's tell Him that today during our payer time. Let's tell Him we trust Him.

In order to trust Jesus, we have to be ALL IN.
Am I all in? Who in my life,
can I share my trust in Jesus with?

Proverbs 3:5-6

Trust in the Lord with all your heart and lean not on your own understanding; in all your ways submit to him, and he will make your paths straight.

Let's see what Isaiah has to say about trust.

There is actually a lot of trust and reassurance going on in this chapter.

Here, he was talking about God's protection for everyone who believed in him and accepted His word. So he used dramatic symbols of danger to make all that clear. God was promising to take care of those who returned to him.

"When you walk through the fire you will not be burned." There will be "dramatic" things happen to you. That is as honest as I can be. Have you ever noticed how something "happens" to a friend and you think they may have overreacted? But…. That same thing "happens" to you and it's the worst time of your life. Our trust in Jesus will help us through both situations. As a disciple and friend you will be a calming effect to a friend in need. As a believer who has a relationship with Jesus, He will be a calming presence to you.

At this point in the story there were those who needed to have the faith to leave captivity in Babylon and make the difficult trip back to Jerusalem and Judah to reestablish the nation of Israel.

Isaiah was trying to build trust in them with him and with God. How is your trust in God?

Do I overreact when "tough"
things happen in my life?
How can I trust Jesus has this under control?

_____

_____

_____

_____

_____

_____

_____

_____

_____

_____

Isaiah 43:2

When you pass through the waters, I will be with you; and when you pass through the rivers, they will not sweep over you. When you walk through the fire, you will not be burned; the flames will not set you ablaze.

One of the final verses from Paul in Philippians.

Paul was encouraging the new believers, to trust in God. He was confident that God would meet their needs because they were so generous to him. Now, let's be clear here. This was not an assurance of an easy life, or life of wealth. What we "need" is determined by God.

What we "need" and what we want are not always the same thing. God tends to bless those who will use the resources they have according to his purposes. This was something Paul saw happening with the Philippians.

I want us to make sure that we also understand that it is not just about material needs.

We will also be provided everything we need, when we are providing for others on their journey. When we trust in Jesus, He will absolutely help us, help others.

We will never lack, with Jesus as our provider. We just have to trust in Him.

Do I truly understand God will meet
all my earthly needs?
What are some things He provides me with?

_____

_____

_____

_____

_____

_____

_____

_____

_____

_____

_____

Philippians 4:19
And my God will meet all your needs according to the riches of his
glory in Jesus Christ.

I have a really deep trust, that my faith and my relationship with Jesus will lead to eternal life, with Him.

v28 *And now, dear children, continue in Him, so that when He appears we may be confident and unashamed before Him at His coming.*

For us I believe that all of this points to our trust. Trust what we learn together. Have confidence to speak and to teach other people what we've learned about Him. Spread it throughout the whole world, one person at a time, if that's what it takes. Over the years, I've spent time thinking about my trust in Jesus. Yes, it's "easy" to say that I trust Him with EVERYTHING. And..... I think I do. But honestly, there are times that things come up in my life, that I "catch" myself trying to manage, or taking action because I "know" what's best. And I realize that I have not fully trusted Him or surrendered that part of my life. That is all part of our individual journey.

- We need to put our trust in His powerful hands.
- We can and should trust the story that we learn from, The Bible.
- We get to trust our beautiful relationship. We get to trust that as a Christian, we have eternal life with Him in heaven. He LOVES us to the moon and back! 😊😊😊😊💜💜💜💜

Like a million x a million times. He's got my trust! Who's with me?

Are there things in my life I have not fully surrendered to Jesus? What are they?

_____

_____

_____

_____

_____

_____

_____

_____

_____

_____

1 John 2: 23-25

No one who denies the Son has the Father; whoever acknowledges the Son has the Father also. As for you, see that what you have heard from the beginning remains in you. If it does, you will also remain in the Son and in the Father. And this is what He promised us—eternal life.

So, to kind of follow up from yesterday... You say you trust Jesus, but as I admitted to you yesterday, something happens in our lives, and all of a sudden we have doubt creep into our head...

Is it a sin to doubt?

So, it is not a sin to struggle with questions of who God is and what it means to belong to him. Those are pretty natural questions that anyone who is seeking God will ask. In this instance James was condemning an attitude that questions whether or not God and his word can be trusted.

It's this wavering in our trust, that blocks our request for wisdom.

It's not so much that God keeps anything from us... when our faith is shaky, we are not prepared to recognize His answers to our questions. Without a foundation of trust in God, we often don't recognize the answers that He gives.

That is why yesterday's question was so important. We have to trust in Him. Remember God wants us!!! He really wants us to join Him in His kingdom.

Can I point to a time in my life
where my trust in God was shaky?

_____

_____

_____

_____

_____

_____

_____

_____

_____

_____

James 1:6-8

But when you ask, you must believe and not doubt, because the one who doubts is like a wave of the sea, blown and tossed by the wind. That person should not expect to receive anything from the Lord. Such a person is double-minded and unstable in all they do.

Wrapping up trust today! Do we really truly have trust in Jesus? What does that look like?

Let's look to Jeremiah for a little friendly advice to close out trust for the week. He grew up in a small town near Jerusalem. He was called on by God to be a prophet when he was very young. He struggled to understand what God's plan was for his life but kind of figured it out on his journey. His nation was being torn down morally, during the time he shared this with us.

So let's look back at those questions from the beginning...

I believe it's one of those head / heart type of things. There's that gap again... between our head and our heart. We might think it with our brain, but until He's in our heart, it's just not quite the same. That is where feeling blessed comes from!

And what does it mean to be blessed, anyway? To be blessed is to be happy or full of joy. But even that doesn't quite get to it, because it's even much more than a feeling. It's like this amazing state we "GET TO" live in, or live with, because of our relationship with Jesus.

I know sometimes it's really hard. School, friends, parents, etc... there is a ton coming at you guys. Trust Him with everything. Talk to him every day. Tell Him how much you love Him! I'm sure He'd love to hear from you! Have an AMAZING day everyone!

What is the difference between
trusting with my heart or my head?
How has this week helped with my trust in Jesus?

Jeremiah 17: 7-8

But blessed is the one who trusts in the Lord, whose confidence is in Him. They will be like a tree planted by the water that sends out its roots by the stream. It does not fear when heat comes; it's leaves are always green. It has no worries in a year of drought and never fails to bear fruit.

Transformation

Our spiritual journey will consist of a lot of change. Hopefully, we will be continuous learners and strengthen our relationship with Jesus as we begin to spend more time with Him. Take a few minutes and think about what that transformation looked like in the beginning of your journey... think about what it looks like for you right now. In today's verse, Paul is speaking to the Romans about change:

Paul is urging them not to simply comply with the current thinking, and way of life. How often are we guilty of that today? Giving in to popular decisions vs doing the right thing? The renewing of our mind that Paul refers to is the kind of transformation that we go through as we grow closer to God. As we become more consistent in our time spent with Him, we'll begin to recognize and understand His will more easily. This continuing transformation, will allow us to push back against the pressures and sin we face today. Spiritual transformation is a life changing event, and a daily part of our journey.

Have I felt a transforming change
in my life because of accepting Jesus?
Do I have a tough time giving in
to the popular choice vs what is right?

_____

_____

_____

_____

_____

_____

_____

_____

_____

Romans 12:2

Do not conform to the pattern of this world, but be transformed by the renewing of your mind. Then you will be able to test and approve what God's will is—His good, pleasing and perfect will.

Fill in the blank.

- I wish I could_____.
- I'm going to_____.
- I want to_____.

Statements that start like this probably all require us to make some sort of change or take some sort of action. In the book of Colossians, Paul is writing to believers who were facing obstacles from false teachers. He wanted to remind them that their growing knowledge of Jesus' teachings are the true path. The true transformation.

Do you see the transformation Paul is talking about? Do you see the action the Colossians had taken in their lives? Focus on the words renewed, knowledge, and image. As Christians, we change things in our lives... as we gain knowledge and get to know Jesus... which helps us to live a more Christ-like life. He created us in His image. Genesis 1:26. The transformation is continuous. As we grow in knowledge, we grow closer to Him. We make different decisions because we begin to understand His will for us.

How does knowing that I am
created in God's image make me feel?
What changes can I make in my life
as I grow closer to Jesus?

_____
_____
_____
_____
_____
_____
_____
_____
_____
_____

Colossians 3:9-10

Do not lie to each other, since you have taken off your old self with its practices and have put on the new self, which is being renewed in knowledge in the image of its creator.

Timing is everything. I'm sure you've heard the phrase before, and maybe you've actually referenced it in your own life. Some opportunity comes into your life and you just aren't ready for it. Or you are more than ready but the opportunity just doesn't present itself.

You see, EVERYONE needs a Savior. Jesus died for us. We are sinners. We don't deserve His grace, yet He makes it available to all of us. We just have to make a few changes. 😊🖤

The transformation we go through is kind of like that also. I accepted Jesus as my Lord and Savior very late in life compared to most Christians. Why did it take me so long? I don't really know. I can tell you for certain that it wasn't because He didn't love me... or want me. I know now that He loves and wants all of us to be with Him. I guess I just wasn't ready.

God loves us so much that He sent Jesus to die on the cross for our salvation. Our eternal life is just waiting for us. (Romans 6:23)

All we have to do is accept Him into our heart. (Romans 10:10) The beautiful thing about God is... He is never late. He's always there at just the right time... when we need Him most. We have to remember it is His will, not ours. We should understand... whenever that time is for each of us to say yes... it is just the beginning. Transformation is a life journey. Accepting Jesus is different than living with Jesus. That comes as we grow with Him. Our transformation is not a sign-up process... it is not a one-time event... it's a life-long commitment.

Have I accepted Jesus into my heart?
How can I help someone else
get to know Jesus as a disciple?

_____

_____

_____

_____

_____

_____

_____

_____

_____

Romans 5:6

You see, at just the right time, when we were still powerless, Christ died for the ungodly.

Want to quench your thirst forever?! Sign me up. 🙋 Today's verse comes from the story where the Samaritan Woman encounters Jesus at the well. (John 4:1-26)

v7. When a Samaritan woman came to draw water, Jesus said to her, "Will you give me a drink?"

She was surprised and questioned his request, because Jews and Samaritans did not associate with one another.

v10. Jesus answered her, "If you knew the gift of God and who it is that asks for a drink, you would have asked Him and He would have given you living water." The woman did not understand that Jesus was referring to her spiritual thirst (spiritual needs). Then in v13-14 Jesus tells her about living water.

This water gives us new life. It is part of our transformation. AND THEN, our transformation provides more water. In John 7:37-39, Jesus makes it clear, this water is the Holy Spirit. Once we accept Jesus as our Lord and Savior and remain in constant contact with Him, our transformation begins. Then, once we become fruitful, we can help others quench their spiritual thirst.

Am I spiritually thirsty?
How do I quench that thirst?
Read my bible? Spend time with friends?

_____

_____

_____

_____

_____

_____

_____

_____

_____

John 4:13-14

Jesus answered, "Everyone who drinks this water will be thirsty again, but whoever drinks the water I give them will never thirst. Indeed, the water I give them will become in them a spring of water welling up to eternal life."

There are many different ways our transformation continues after we accept Jesus. Prayer is a very important part of that continuous change. Paul was a man that prayed a lot. He had confidence in His communication with God. Today we look at Paul's second letter to the Thessalonians. In this part of the letter—2 Thessalonians 3:1-5—Paul has requested prayers.

v4-5 We have confidence in the Lord that you are doing well and will continue to do things we command. May the Lord direct your hearts into God's love and Christ's perseverance.

The Lord gives us belief in what we are doing. As we continue our journey of transformation, we will grow into a greater understanding of the love God has for us.

Paul was a man who was committed to a prayerful relationship with God. Part of our trans*form*ation is our prayer life. Praying to God for Him to continue to "form" us like clay, as it states in Isaiah 64:8. We want God to continually work in our lives, molding us, like a piece of clay, to be more like Jesus. God is so masterful! We have a lot of work to do also, but let's all pray for Him to continue to work on us and through us to help others. I pray that He continues to smooth out our rough edges like that piece of clay. ♥☺

Have I prayed to God for Him to show me His will for my life?

_____

_____

_____

_____

_____

_____

_____

_____

2 Thessalonians 3:1–5

Finally, brethren, pray for us, that the word of the Lord may run swiftly and be glorified, just as it is with you, and that we may be delivered from unreasonable and wicked men; for not all have faith. But the Lord is faithful, who will establish you and guard you from the evil one. And we have confidence in the Lord concerning you, both that you do and will do the things we command you. Now may the Lord direct your hearts into the love of God and into the patience of Christ.

What does it mean to repent? Are repentance and transformation the same thing? Today's verse comes from the very beginning of Jesus' public ministry.

The simple way to describe repentance would be "ask for forgiveness." But, I feel there's a little more to it than that. We must take responsibility for ALL our actions.

Here are a few more good questions to ask ourselves. Do we have true regret for what we've done wrong? Are we committed to NOT doing it again? And remember forgiveness is a two way street. So, as we are asking for forgiveness for our actions, we need to be prepared to give it freely also.

Repentance is not the same as transformation, but it certainly is part of our transformation. It is when we allow God to transform us from the inside.

Transformation requires us to change. Think of it as training ourselves to live a different life, a life with Jesus at the center of everything we do. Matthew 4:19. *Jesus said, "Follow me and I will make you fishers of men."* The phrase "I will make you," tells us that Jesus had to mold them. Just like He wants to mold us today. But, just as those first disciples did, we have to allow Him into our hearts for our transformation to begin.

Have I made room in my heart for Jesus?

_____
_____
_____
_____
_____
_____
_____
_____
_____
_____
_____

Matthew 4:17
From that time on Jesus began to preach, "Repent, for the kingdom of heaven has come near."

Let's add a little more on to yesterday. The KJV of Acts 3:19 is a little different from the NIV... *Repent ye therefore, and be converted, that your sins may be blotted out, when the times of refreshing shall come from the presence of the Lord.*

Repent and be converted (Transformed)

Turn to God so that the transformation process can begin. If we truly repent we will change the way we do things, the way we act. If we truly convert, we will be saved. Without repentance, our transformation cannot take place.

NIV... so that your sins may be wiped out...

KJV... that your sins may be blotted out...

Both versions refer to our sins being erased completely due to our repentance. Then the transformation truly begins... then times of refreshing may come from the Lord. Our refreshing comes from spending time with Jesus.

At first we are born of the flesh, but after our transformation, we become born of the Spirit. Our refreshing is a constant part of our journey. Let's make our refreshing a daily routine. A daily part of our transformation.

Is my time with Jesus, a daily routine for me?
If it's not, what do I need to change
to make it a routine?

_____

_____

_____

_____

_____

_____

_____

_____

_____

_____

Acts 3:19

Repent, then, and turn to God, so that your sins may be wiped out,
that times of refreshing may come from the Lord.

Calling

What is a calling? Have you been called? What was your answer?

What will your answer be? Let's look at Paul's description to Timothy.

We are saved because Jesus took our sin to the cross. We are not saved because we've done anything to be worthy of it. We are saved because of Jesus' worthiness. He was the PERFECT sacrifice. It was His blood that saved us. His life for ours. We are saved to become children of God.

We are called to a holy life. That's a pretty powerful statement! But... you cannot let it scare you. A holy life does not mean that it has to be perfect. Oh sure, that would be amazing if we could do that, but you and I both know that's not really possible.

The most important part of living a holy life, is living our life for God. As His children, although still sinful, we are "set apart" for His work. God wants us to be faithful to Him and be His disciples, His workers! 💜👣🙏😊

Look at Paul and Timothy. Both were saved and received a calling. They were called into ministry to serve others. The "things" we do, don't save us. We "do" the things we do because we are saved.

Our calling comes from God because of our acceptance of Jesus into our hearts. Loving Jesus changes ones heart. So, are you ready for the most important call of your life? Don't let it go to voicemail. 💜😊

Have I felt a calling in my life?

2 Timothy 1:9

He has saved us and called us to a holy life—not because of anything we have done but because of his own purpose and grace. This grace was given us in Christ Jesus before the beginning of time.

Just in case we ever get too big for our shoes on our journey with Jesus, He gives us a little reminder about how we fit in to the plan, and what His plans are for us.

Jesus chose them. Being able to walk with Jesus and be in relationship with Him gave the disciples great understanding. The purpose for that understanding was for them to bear fruit. Follow up and continue what Jesus had started.

We've talked about how special that relationship must have been. They got to literally walk with Jesus! ♥👍 But..... Jesus did leave them... when He ascended. And guess what? He left them with the Holy Spirit. They still had continual contact with Him through their prayer communication.

Just like the disciples, we should remain in constant contact with Jesus! He's called us to continue what He started. How can we help Him, how can we understand what He wants us to do next, if we don't talk to Him?

We do have to say yes and accept Jesus into our hearts. But make no mistake... He chose us. He chose us to work. He chose us to follow His lead! He chose us to continue being disciples for Him.

How special does that make you feel? Ok, I've got to go, I've got to take this call. It's VERY important. ♥😊👍

How does it make me feel
knowing that God chose me?

_____

_____

_____

_____

_____

_____

_____

_____

_____

_____

_____

John 15:16

You did not choose me, but I chose you and appointed you so that you might go and bear fruit—fruit that will last—and so that whatever you ask in my name the Father will give you.

Our calling can be confusing. It will possibly be difficult for us to understand. There's like this tug-o-war going on in our heads. If we've said yes to God, then we are comfortable knowing we are saved. But... we also know we are not perfect. Paul gives us some pretty good advice today.

Paul gives us a great vision, here, of a runner. He understands that what is ahead of him is what's most important. Past mistakes are EXACTLY that—PAST...

Paul is referring to his calling of bringing the good news of Jesus to the whole world. He can't do that work.. WE can't do that work, if we are constantly turning around.

If you are having a tough time letting go and moving forward, focusing on the work we have to do, I suggest spending a little more time with Jesus. Start living your life for Him. Remember, in the beginning you may have to really work at setting aside time for Him. But over time, it will become more and more important to you as you realize how much He has in store for you. He wants to move forward with you!

You may use something from your past as a life lesson to look back on, but besides that, let it go, and move on!! We don't have time for that! Can you see what's ahead of us? We've got work to do! Yes.... YOU and I have A LOT of work to do!!

Do I tend to focus on what is ahead of me,
or do I get stuck in the past?
How can I do a better job of living my life for Jesus?

_____
_____
_____
_____
_____
_____
_____
_____
_____
_____

Philippians 3:12-14

Not that I have already obtained all this, or have already arrived at my goal, but I press on to take hold of that for which Christ Jesus took hold of me. Brothers and sisters, I do not consider myself yet to have taken hold of it. But one thing I do: Forgetting what is behind and straining toward what is ahead, I press on toward the goal to win the prize for which God has called me heavenward in Christ Jesus.

Thank you God for choosing us.
For calling us to serve you. 🖤

In this letter, Paul gives thanks for what God is doing in their lives.
Being chosen as firstfruits could be intimidating for sure. It definitely
sets up the expectations for them.

Those expectations may cause some of us to just simply crumble,
because they are so great. Others will put on those "good news"
shoes and get to work.

That is why our 15 minute beginning was/is so important. Our
relationship with Jesus is a building process. You have to begin a
relationship with Him before He will reveal your purpose. If and when
we commit our life to Jesus, He will do AMAZING things through us.
The calling to serve Him is so great! He will use you in the most perfect
of ways, at times that you don't even realize it's happening.

There are times that the work will be hard, but He will ALWAYS guide
us through. On days when I know I have to get some writing done, but
I'm a little tired, unfocused, etc.... I picture Him rolling up His sleeves
with me and giving me encouragement to do His work. Remember,
although He's called us, He is also going to provide for us. We will have
all the tools we need to do the job!! So we should be thankful that He
called us, but also give ongoing praise as He continues to provide for
us! 🖤☺

In my prayers today, what things
can I thank God for doing in my life?
How do I feel God has used me in the past?

---

2 Thessalonians 2:13-14

But we ought always to thank God for you, brothers and sisters loved by the Lord, because God chose you as firstfruits to be saved through the sanctifying work of the Spirit and through belief in the truth. He called you to this through our gospel, that you might share in the glory of our Lord Jesus Christ.

Are we all looking to expand our fellowship? Our calling can and should result in that expansion.

Have you ever thought about your journey like this….. being in fellowship with Jesus. In the verses leading up to v9 Paul reminds us to be thankful for ALL of the things we have received in Christ Jesus. We have received everything we need to grow our Family of Christians.

Look at the verse one more time. God has CALLED us to fellowship with His Son. What will our response be to that call? That is the BIG question.

Fellowship = associating with people who share the same interest. Are we answering our call? Are we sharing Jesus and expanding that fellowship? Or, are we keeping Jesus all to ourselves?

God is Faithful... the beginning of the verse is reminding us that we DO and we WILL always have everything we need from our amazing Father. We gain knowledge through His word and we all have any number of spiritual gifts to help us fellowship with others.

That sharing process, of answering our calling, creates the relationships needed to grow our Christian family. Think about things in your life that you've been excited about and just had to tell EVERYBODY! THAT is what answering the call could look like. Telling EVERYONE about the greatest news EVER! Let's spread the word!

Am I excited about sharing Jesus?

_____
_____
_____
_____
_____
_____
_____
_____
_____
_____
_____
_____

1 Corinthians 1:9
God is faithful, who has called you into fellowship with his Son, Jesus Christ our Lord.

If you are going to answer your calling, you have to know what your calling is, right? I mean... how much sense does that make? Well... how exactly do you find that out? YES!! You just said it didn't you. You have to be in prayer about it! He will most certainly light your path AND give you EVERYTHING you need! Just ask Him!! That is why our relationship with Him is so important.

Sometimes it gets confusing. It seems so hard. I'm sure many people think, gosh I'm too scared to speak in front of people. I really love Jesus, but I'm nervous about sharing. There are so many other gifts than teaching. It gets confusing for us because we try to choose what we think is important, or what WE WANT to do vs asking God what He wants us to do. That's the key! It is not about you or me, it's about God!!

If you look at the word ministry, it involves so many different things....

Romans 12:1-8 He has a purpose for each and every one of us! He knows what He needs us to do, how He wants us to do it, and when we need to do it!

Are you are willing to be a living sacrifice to God, and be an example for others to follow..... yes?

All you have to do is ask Him. He'll tell you!

Have I asked God what He wants me to do?

_____
_____
_____
_____
_____
_____
_____
_____
_____
_____
_____
_____

Romans 8:28
And we know that in all things God works for the good of those who love him, who have been called according to his purpose.

I can't do it. I can't be perfect. I can't be holy. It is just too much pressure to follow Jesus. Here's the deal; I agree. Today's verses can be very intimidating. Some may read them and become discouraged. We need to look at it differently.

Today's verse may make you think God requires perfection, as soon as you accept Him and from that point forward. How many Christians do you know who are perfect? I'll wait while you think... Yes, that's the same answer I got... 0! So then, what does today's reading mean?

Does being holy require us to be perfect, which is something we can never live up to? I don't believe God would have called us to something He knows we cannot achieve.

To be holy is to be devoted, to be set apart for God's purpose. As holy individuals WE ARE CALLED TO CHANGE OUR BEHAVIORS. We need to think better thoughts... make better choices... live like we have Christ in us. We GET TO be an example for others. People do what people see! We have a standard set for us by Jesus. As His followers, we need to be better than we were yesterday, because that's what we GET TO do! 🤍😊

Don't focus on what you can't do!! Focus on what you GET TO do. You GET TO be different, you GET TO focus on a NEW you.

We are called to be set apart. When you think of being holy, be better than you were yesterday. It is something we should all strive for. Let's continue to focus on making Jesus the CENTER of our lives!

What things can I focus on tomorrow
that will make me better than I was today?
Do I feel pressure to be perfect?

_____

_____

_____

_____

_____

_____

_____

_____

_____

_____

1 Peter 1:15-16

But just as he who called you is holy, so be holy in all you do; for it is written: "Be holy, because I am holy."

Fruitfulness

Let's focus this week on what it means to be fruitful. If a tree is fruitful, it means it is productive. It produces much fruit. Let's compare that to being a Christian. If we are fruitful, we will produce better results... in our life and in the lives of others. So, how do we do that?

We need to plant ourselves by the water. We need to spend time in God's word. How much time? How about starting out with 15 minutes a day, EVERY day! I know you think time is hard to come by, but honestly I could find 15 minutes for you, without even knowing how you spend your time. It really comes down to committing the time EVERY day; making time with Him the most important time of each and EVERY day!

So there are two parts to being fruitful.

1. If we are in God's word (planted by the water), we will gain strength and survive any droughts we may encounter in our spiritual life.
2. We can help others do the same and grow our family of believers.

Are you ready to commit that time to Jesus? Honestly, you will find that when you are consistent with 15 minutes, you'll want to spend even more time with Him!

What does being fruitful mean?

_____

_____

_____

_____

_____

_____

_____

_____

_____

_____

_____

Jeremiah 17: 7-8
But blessed is the one who trusts in the Lord, whose confidence is in Him. They will be like a tree planted by the water that sends out its roots by the stream.

Yesterday, we heard from Jeremiah. Today, let's hear from Jesus.

The vine and the branches...

In v1-4, Jesus is urging His disciples to remain in Him. To be fruitful, they had to rely completely on Him, His teaching, and His way. Today, the power that we have to be fruitful comes to us only if we remain in relationship with Him.

You see, God has a plan for each and every one of us. What He wants us to do... what he wants us to become... will flourish if we stay connected to Jesus (the vine)! Staying connected to the vine, makes us one with Jesus. If we are not connected to Him, we are nothing more than a dead branch.

We have to stay connected to our power source, just like the disciples 2,000 years ago.

How can we stay connected to the vine?

Prayer, reading our Bible, daily devotionals, this text, going to church, attending youth events, sharing Him with others... as we've discussed many times, all of these ways are great. The thing we have to ask ourselves is... Are we consistently making time to stay connected to The Vine?

What am I doing to stay connected to the Vine?
How consistent am I with
spending time with Jesus?

_____

_____

_____

_____

_____

_____

_____

_____

_____

_____

John 15:5

I am the vine; you are the branches. If you remain in me and I in you, you will bear much fruit; apart from me you can do nothing.

Being fruitful will give us an inner peace and an outward joy that cannot be matched!

Think about the times you've helped someone, or worked on different mission projects. When we do good, we feel good. But, let's make sure we also understand who is guiding us, who is helping us help others.

There are many times fruitfulness in my life has given me a little extra spring in my step or has made my smile a little bigger... and that's ok. But, we need to understand that the real reason to be fruitful is to bring glory to God!

The Father is pleased when we carry out the teachings of Jesus. We have to remember that Jesus not only taught us how to live, but he lived that life also. He modeled the expectations for us.

The real intent in being fruitful should be to bring glory to God—not the disciple. As the vine cares for the tree, our Father cares for us. Bearing fruit, spreading His word, caring for others, bringing people into our heavenly family here on earth, brings glory to God who cares for us.

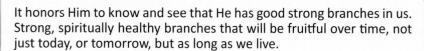

It honors Him to know and see that He has good strong branches in us. Strong, spiritually healthy branches that will be fruitful over time, not just today, or tomorrow, but as long as we live.

Being fruitful is a commitment. A commitment to being in consistent relationship with Jesus to bring Glory to our Father.

Are the things I'm doing in my life
bringing glory to God? Why? Why not?

_____

_____

_____

_____

_____

_____

_____

_____

_____

_____

John 15:8
This is to my Father's glory, that you bear much fruit, showing
yourselves to be my disciples.

So, let's say we understand what it means to be fruitful. Another question may be, what is the fruit of the Spirit?

Lets look at it like this. The verse describes the characteristics of someone who is in a relationship with God. The Spirit produces this in us. It is the result of our relationship with Jesus over time. It takes time for a tree to produce fruit, just like it takes time for us, as believers, to have this fruit in our lives. We have to mature as Christians. That is why you always hear our relationship with Jesus referred to as a journey.

I wanted to look at fruitfulness from this perspective, because I want you to understand that these characteristics are all things that help us be fruitful. As we walk with Jesus every day, we become more mature... we understand things in greater detail. We have moments that we see them in action.

Then, as the fruit of the Spirit grows in our lives, we can become even more fruitful.

What is one thing I can do today,
or this week, to share Jesus?

Galatians 5:22-23
But the fruit of the Spirit is love, joy, peace, forbearance, kindness, goodness, faithfulness, gentleness and self control. Against such things there is no law.

Can anyone be fruitful? Well, that all depends. Go to Mark chapter 4 and read the parable of the sower. Go ahead, read the entire story.

This parable teaches us a few things about the ability for seeds to grow in our life. It teaches us that the gospel will not be received the same way by everyone, which means that it will not grow the same in everyone either. There are four examples, for us here. In each of the first three examples, something gets in the way.

1. Resistance from sin; Satan takes it away.
2. Oppression from others. With no root, the word slips away.
3. Worries of the world. Things get in the way and choke the word out.

Now look at today's verse. If the word does take root, it produces a fruitful life. Look at the words in the verse; hear, accept, and produce. They are action words in present tense. It is ALL about the strength of our relationship with Jesus. If our relationship is strong, we hear God's word, and accept it. Our transformation produces fruitfulness.

So, we obviously want to be the fourth example. We not only hear the word, but we share it with others and help them understand it. Some of us may not produce the numbers in the verse, some of us may help even more. The important thing is to help guide as many people as we can into the Kingdom of Heaven. That's what being fruitful is all about.

Is there anything getting in the way of my spiritual growth?

Mark 4:20

Others like seed grown on good soil, hear the word, accept it, and produce a crop—some thirty, some sixty, some a hundred times what was sown.

Honestly, I was a pretty good kid. I didn't get into a whole lot of trouble. But, when I did my father would discipline me. It usually sounded something like this.

You broke the rules, you have to face the consequences. The reason I discipline you is because I love you.

Obviously, I would get mad, because I never thought the punishment "fit the crime," and many times I didn't think I should be punished at all. I didn't really care about what he had to say back then, but I understand things a whole lot better now. Most times I learned a lesson from that discipline. Lessons that I think about to this day. In fact, I share them with my boys so they don't have to learn the lesson the same way I did. 😊💜

If we think about it, God's discipline is the same.

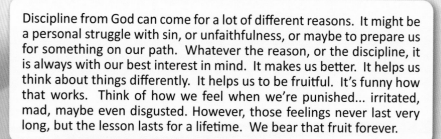

Discipline from God can come for a lot of different reasons. It might be a personal struggle with sin, or unfaithfulness, or maybe to prepare us for something on our path. Whatever the reason, or the discipline, it is always with our best interest in mind. It makes us better. It helps us think about things differently. It helps us to be fruitful. It's funny how that works. Think of how we feel when we're punished... irritated, mad, maybe even disgusted. However, those feelings never last very long, but the lesson lasts for a lifetime. We bear that fruit forever.

what things do I already do, on a daily basis,
that show fruitfulness in me?

_____

_____

_____

_____

_____

_____

_____

_____

_____

_____

Hebrews 12:11

No discipline seems pleasant at the time, but painful. Later on,
however, it produces a harvest of righteousness and peace for those
who have been trained by it.

In today's verse Jesus is reminding the disciples that He not only chose them, but also reminded them why.

God chose us too! He chose us to be His children. When we allow Him to work in our lives, He gives us a new heart. (Ezekiel 36:26) He has appointed us to bear fruit. As we remain in His word and share Jesus with others, our relationship becomes stronger. Those Christ like characteristics from Galatians 5:22-23, become part of us. We can see them in action every day in our lives and how we influence the lives of others.

You see, God chooses us, but we have to allow Jesus to work through us, to make more disciples and to continue to bring people into the Kingdom. As those characteristics grow in us, they increase our ability to be fruitful.

Remember the parable from the other day? It's important to remember that here. As our relationship with Jesus gets stronger, the seeds we plant will grow stronger also. We will begin to produce fruit that will last.

How does it make me feel, knowing God chose me?
Knowing He chose me,
does it make me want to live differently?

_____

_____

_____

_____

_____

_____

_____

_____

_____

John 15:16

You did not choose me, but I chose you and appointed you so that you might go and bear fruit—fruit that will last—and so that whatever you ask in my name the father will give you.

Perseverance

POSSIBLE

I'll show them. I'll repay them for what they did. I'll get even. Those are phrases or feelings I'm sure many of us have expressed. Revenge is often our immediate thought when someone wrongs us in some way. Is that really how we should respond as followers of Jesus? Let's see what Paul has to say about perseverance:

Listening to Paul's advice here can be difficult. Most times we immediately think... how can I get back at that person. We have that "built-in reflex" for revenge. Honestly, the plan for revenge can consume us. We build up hatred and it just eats at us... we say it's not a big deal, but we just can't let it go. I know, because I've been there. I've really worked hard to turn those feelings around.

Jesus set an AMAZING example for us here. Even as He was suffering on the cross, He said, "Father forgive them for they know not what they do." Ok, I need you to replay that again... while Jesus was suffering, He gave forgiveness to the very people who nailed Him to that cross! We must follow His example.

I know sometimes people can do awful things to us, or say terrible things about us. But... we will never have to endure the suffering and humiliation that Jesus did... He did it all for us. Knowing that... thinking about that... closing my eyes and hearing Him forgive them... we can get through anything.

Do I have a reflex for revenge?
What can I do to change that?

_____

_____

_____

_____

_____

_____

_____

_____

POSSIBLE

Romans 12:17-18

Do not repay anyone evil for evil. Be careful to do what is right in the eyes of everyone. If it is possible, as far as it depends on you, live at peace with everyone.

Can my faith help with my perseverance? Of course it can, and it does. Sometimes we might not even realize it.

We all have sinful things in our lives we may struggle with. But, think about all the bad things we instinctively already stay away from. Sure, some of it has to do with the foundation that our parents set for us. And if we have a good group of people in our circle, that will help us too. But, there will be times we will have to pray harder about something... ask Jesus to give us strength and guidance.

Overcoming the world, to me, means persevering over temptations that are put in our path. There are times we have to fight to free ourselves from sinful impulses. Jesus fought for us, right?! He defeated Satan on the cross. That, by itself, should give us the perseverance to get through anything. Just knowing how much He loves us. He wants to and will help us with any battle we have to fight. But to have His help, He has to be part of our life. Do you talk to Him every day, or just on the bad days? Do you thank Him for the food and shelter He provided for you today? We have to focus on spending time with Him EVERY day! To persevere in this world, we need to have faith in Jesus. In order to have faith in Jesus, we have to know Him.

What temptations do I deal with in my life?
What things can I do to fight them?

_____

_____

_____

_____

_____

_____

_____

_____

_____

POSSIBLE

1 John 5:5

Who is it that overcomes the world? Only the one who believes that
Jesus is the Son of God.

Have you ever needed a good pep talk to help you get through something? To help you persevere? Let's see what Paul says to Timothy in today's verse.

So, we know Paul was Timothy's friend and mentor. Timothy was having a tough time of it, trying to lead the church in Ephesus after Paul left. False teachers threatened to destroy what Paul had established.

There are going to be times in our lives that doing the right thing may seem difficult... where being Christ-like takes a great amount of courage. We may meet people who do not believe in Jesus and who may even want to challenge our views and beliefs. When we encounter those instances, we have to think about our relationship with Jesus... think about how much He loves us and what He's done for us.

Sometimes the journey may be difficult. Sometimes we may have questions. We can gain strength and wisdom from our circle of believers. It's important to fight the good fight of our faith, to keep a firm grip on our belief. Paul gave Timothy some sound advice, which is relevant for us too.

Who in my life has given me one of those pep talks? How helpful am I in giving pep talks to others?

_____

_____

_____

_____

_____

_____

_____

_____

_____

_____

POSSIBLE

1 Timothy 6:12

Fight the good fight of the faith. Take hold of the eternal life to which you were called when you made your good confession in the presence of many witnesses.

Jesus is the Light of the world! His light will help us get through anything.

In John 1:5, Jesus is the light. Darkness symbolizes the sin we have in our lives and the possible sin that is in our future path. Light always wins over darkness.

What do you do, when the power goes off in your house? You grab a flashlight or a candle, right? Oh, ok, I forgot, you can use your phone too. 😄🤍 My point is, when you are in that situation you need some kind of light to see.

So what does this mean for us in our relationship with Jesus? Think about all the darkness, all the evil Jesus faced. Think about all the times Satan tried to challenge Jesus' light, even getting Judas to betray Jesus and give Him up to the Roman soldiers, who crucified Him. Even then, the Light of Jesus prevailed over darkness as sin was conquered by our Savior.

Think about the darkness we face today. The sin we are surrounded by. Some days it seems like it meets us at every corner. How can we possibly resist all of it?

Well, we will win with the Light of Jesus.

It's so important for us to have the Light of Jesus in us, and for us to take it with us everywhere we go. When we walk with Jesus, we walk in His light. When we have the Light of Jesus, we can prevail over any darkness. #ETERNALLIGHT

Am I carrying the light of Jesus with me?
Everywhere?

John 1:5
The light shines in the darkness and the darkness has not overcome it.

Knowing The Word is extremely important for our perseverance!

Even today we can encounter false teachers or people who may try to manipulate scripture. In some cases, it's as easy as changing a few words to distort the true meaning.

For us to verify the message, we have to spend time in the Bible. I'm thinking 15 minutes a day would be a great start. 😊💜

As Christians, we should be aware of false teaching, but we should not be afraid of it. In fact, if the opportunity presents itself, we should be eager to present the truth. Remember, as Jesus told us in John 14:6, I am the way, the truth, and the life. No one comes to the Father except through me.

Being in relationship with Jesus, spending time with Him, in our Bible, will equip us with the perseverance needed to handle anyone who wants to challenge our faith. Knowledge of the word will also help us bring others into our family of believers.

Do I spend daily time in God's word?
How often do I read something,
and then share it with others?

_____

_____

_____

_____

_____

_____

_____

_____

_____

POSSIBLE

1 John 4: 1,4

v1 Dear friends, do not believe every spirit, but test the spirits to see whether they are from God, because many false prophets have gone out into the world... v4. You, dear children, are from God and have overcome them, because the one who is in you is greater than the one who is in the world.

Have you ever been afraid to face something? How much do you worry about sinful things? If you are afraid, of anything, having a relationship with Jesus should give you strength... a strength that would make superheros shake in their shoes.

We've already won the battles we may face, because Jesus is the ultimate conqueror.

Jesus won against evil for ALL of us!! He is our Savior. The battles we face are nothing because we have the love and strength of Jesus in us. As Jesus' family members, we have the comfort of knowing He's ALWAYS got our back. He's with us EVERY step of the way. Our strength, our perseverance, is in our Lord and Savior. It is a bond that cannot be separated! It is a strength that cannot be broken!

What are the things in life that I fear most?
How does the strength of Jesus
help me face those things?

_____

_____

_____

_____

_____

_____

_____

_____

_____

POSSIBLE

Romans 8: 37-39

No, in all these things we are more than conquerors through Him
who loved us. For I am convinced that neither death nor life, neither
angels nor demons, neither the present nor the future, nor any
powers, neither height nor depth, nor anything else in all creation,
will be able to separate us from the love of God that is in Christ Jesus
our Lord.

Have you ever gotten tired while running a race? So tired you wanted to quit? But you didn't quit because you knew you couldn't do it. Maybe someone was cheering you on, and you didn't want to let them down. Maybe you didn't want to let yourself down. Hebrews 11 is a strong dose of inspiration for us as we run our path. It shows the faith of some of the greatest people in the Bible. Honestly, it's like a faith hall of fame! Please take a few minutes and read it now, before reading today's verse.

If you EVER have a question or doubt about your faith, when you get tired on your journey, and you will get tired, I encourage you to reread Chapter 11. As you read, picture yourself running your race toward eternal life. Can you visualize all of these heroes of faith cheering you on as you go, passing their encouragement on to you?!

We can receive perseverance from reading about all these great examples in chapter 11, but let's make sure we focus our eyes and our hearts on the most incredible example of perseverance we could EVER ask for—Jesus!

Because of Him our debt has been paid in full. When I think about quitting, I think about Jesus. Then.........I STOP thinking about quitting!

#IMNOTAQUITTER

Who are my biggest cheerleaders? Jesus?
How often am I there to cheer my friends on,
helping them persevere?

POSSIBLE

Hebrews 12:1

Therefore, since we are surrounded by such a great cloud of witnesses, let us throw off everything that hinders and the sin that so easily entangles. And let us run with perseverance the race marked out for us.

Friendship

Let's take a look at friendship this week. What is a true friend? What qualities do they have?

There are four things I want from someone who is a friend of mine.

1. Someone who always has my back!
2. Someone who always has my best interest at heart.
3. Someone that makes me a better person.

Paul is someone that has these qualities. In today's verse Paul is speaking to the believers in Rome.

The fourth thing I want from a friend is someone I can share my faith with. Someone I can talk to about Jesus. I want to share in my friends' journey, but just as important, I want them to share in mine. I want them to pour into me!

Paul says it beautifully in v12... *that you and I may be mutually encouraged by each other's faith*. Paul hopes that he encourages his fellow believers, but he also knows that he needs to be encouraged too.

Have you ever thought about Jesus being your friend? He's always got your back. He always has your best interest in mind. He will most definitely make you a better person.   We just need to spend more time with Jesus.   It's just that simple.

Who are my true friends?
What qualities do they have?

Romans 1:11-12
I long to see you so that I may impart to you some spiritual gift to make you strong— that is, that you and I may be mutually encouraged by each other's faith.

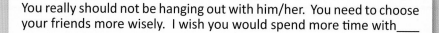

You really should not be hanging out with him/her. You need to choose your friends more wisely. I wish you would spend more time with____ _____.

Sound familiar? There are a lot of people in our lives who want to give us advice on who we should hang out with... our parents, relatives, and even other friends. Well, as difficult as it may be to hear, it's because they love us. And guess what... it REALLY does matter.

Here, Paul is talking to the believers in Corinth, urging them not to listen to non-believers and false teachers because it would affect their character. Guess what, Paul's point is still important today... to people of all ages. Yes, teenagers may be more influenced by peer pressure, but trust me there will always be a little peer pressure in your lives. It will just be about different things when you get older.

As Paul is saying, we can get caught up in the approval from other people, but those people may not want what's best for us. Let's always make sure God's word is the foundation for our decisions. When you are true friends with someone, you get to share a lot with that person, but NOTHING will ever be better than sharing Jesus. #TRUTH

Do I think I always make the best choices about who I spend my time with?

1 Corinthians 15:33

Do not be misled: "Bad company corrupts good character."

How reliable are our friends? Are they ALWAYS there for you, no matter what? Are they closer to you than your own siblings? Does it really matter?

One of the most important things I've discovered on my Christian journey is... if I want to be close to someone, if I want to have them in my circle, have them love me and pour into me, then I have to love them first. It may take a while to get to know me, but once you do, I'm ALL IN! I want to do life with you! I will treat you like a brother or sister, like blood!

I don't want someone to love me because of what I am, or what I've done. I want them to love me because of who I am. I'll ALWAYS try to be a great friend, but there are days I fall short. Will your friends still love you on those days? That's the key!!

And YES, who you spend your time with really does matter. Look at the story of Jesus healing the paralyzed man. Mark 2:1-5

Read it closely. The house was so crowded. They couldn't get to Jesus. The man's friends were so COMMITTED to get him in front of Jesus that they went in through the roof!! Jesus healed the man because of THEIR FAITH... THEIR commitment to their friend and their faith. Would YOU do that for your friends? Would THEY do it for you? Here's the deal, it's NOT about how many friends you have. It's about who your friends are, and how much they love you!

How reliable are my friends?
Do they consider me reliable?
Do people in my life love me because of who I am?

Proverbs 18:24
One who has unreliable friends soon comes to ruin, but there is a friend who sticks closer than a brother.

Let's pick up where we left off yesterday. Something I've realized over the years is that a lot of times family is in, and out. I may talk or text with a family member for a few weeks in a row, and then not text at all for several weeks. My friends though, my really true friends are ALWAYS there. There may be little time lapses over the years, but one of us always picks up the phone eventually. That phone call may come because of a need, or it might just be to catch up. But either way, there is that group of friends I am close to... when things are good or when things are tough. Now I'm not saying that is, or will be anyone else's experience, but it is what today's verse talks about.

Siblings may fight when times are good, but usually they are there for you in times of trouble. They come to your defense if there's gossip. They back you up when you need it most.

Your friends, the people you CHOOSE to have in your life, are like siblings because your tough times will make them love you even more. Times of adversity will bring people closer.

True friends are a constant fountain of love and support. It is so true that family comes together when big things happen, or when tough times hit. But, it's always important to have a strong group of friends also! Friends that you can share everything with, good and bad. But the most important thing to share with each other is Jesus. A great friend will strengthen your relationship with Jesus, just as Jesus will strengthen your friendships.

Who are the people in my life
that are always there for me?
Do I feel that presence from Jesus?

Proverbs 17:17
A friend loves at all times, and a brother is born for a time of adversity.

Hey did you hear about what _____ did?

Does _____ know about it?

Is this some sort of a cover up? No, not at all. This is about us or our friends making mistakes. Certainly I've made my share of them. You will too... and so will your friends. The back half of the verse brings about this question; when you hear about something that one of your friends did, what do you do? Do you squash the gossip and set the record straight or do you immediately think about who you are going to tell the "news" to?

You see, when we love people, we need to love them unconditionally. Love them in spite of their "offense" or mistakes.   That is what fostering love and friendship looks like. Gossiping will just tear close friends apart.

This verse should help us understand, we should not pass on negative stuff about other people. If we hear something about someone else, we should just let the "stuff" stop with us. When / if we help spread the "stuff" it will eventually cause harm to our friendships. So, stop the gossip; spread the love. #greatfriends

What do I really do,
when I hear "stuff" about my friends?

Proverbs 17:9
Whoever would foster love covers an offense, but whoever repeats the matter separates close friends.

I love you like a brother/sister. Love you brother. Love you sister. I'm sure those phrases sound familiar. Those statements, those feelings, are probably reserved for our closest friends! But... we also have to understand we should love EVERYONE! In today's verse, John reminds us of a very important command.

So, I'm going to shoot you straight here. If we love God, we should be able to love EVERYONE else. It is what we "get to" do as Christians. We get to learn how to love from the very best, because He loved us first. Jesus is an AMAZING role model.

Yes, there are people who are closer to us. A group of people in our "circle" that we spend more time with, or have more in common with. Our friends.

But understand, God's expectation is that we love EVERYONE. We should have a kind heart for everyone. We should treat everyone nicely. Look at v20.

Whoever claims to love God yet hates a brother or sister is a liar. WOW!!! That's tough stuff right there. But, you have to consider the size of our family. 😊 🖤

We are ALL God's children. I'll be honest, I didn't get it at first. I'm a work in progress. It is all part of our journey. We will always have special affection for people we call our friends, but we need to love EVERYONE! We should have so much love flowing from us that it makes it impossible to hate. Can you imagine a world, where everyone is your friend?

Do I truly understand the love Jesus has for me?
How can I possibly show love
toward someone who doesn't like me?

1 John 4:21
And He has given us this command: Anyone who loves God must also love their brother and sister.

Ok, you've seen it this week, and I've said it countless other times, so don't roll your eyes. ☺

Who you spend your time with matters. It helps shape who we are and who we'll become. Which leads into one of my favorite verses in the Bible, Proverbs 27:17.

Spending time with the right people will strengthen our faith. It will make us better people. Why? Look back at my criteria for my friends from the first day. I said I want friends that want what's best for me. There's a little bit more to that. Those friends will also want me to be at my best, because that will make them better.

So, you see, in true friendship we make each other better people. When Jesus is part of what we share with our friends we become stronger in our faith. It grows our character.

If we are hanging out with the "wrong" crowd, it can cause our values and beliefs to be weakened, or even worse, cause us to lose our way completely.

Obviously, spending time with people who hold the same values as us (or maybe even stronger than us), will give us the ability to build each other up. True friends will inspire us to be better disciples. They will hold us accountable and challenge us to live Christ-like lives. But more importantly, a true friend expects us to do the same for them.

How can I help my friends strengthen their faith?

_____
_____
_____
_____
_____
_____
_____

I promise, I used to be intimidated by spending time with people who were "better" than me. When I say that, I mean people who may be further along in their journey, or who know more about the Bible than me. And because of where they are at on their journey, you can see they are living differently, and they are loving differently. Their relationship with Jesus is highly visible to me. But guess what, I soon realized that we had A LOT to offer each other. I realized quickly my friendships are a two way street! So, you see, as friends we really do sharpen one another!

Proverbs 27:17
As iron sharpens Iron; So one person sharpens another.

Coming Soon...

From *The Starting Line* to *The Dented Can*... *The Power of Prayer* to *The Spare Tire*... Mark shares stories about the checkpoints that led him to become a Christian and since then have brought understanding to him in his life. Reading his stories is like sitting down to a conversation with Mark. A conversation that will touch your heart, cause you to think, and bring you closer to Jesus as you read about Mark's own *Journey with Jesus*.

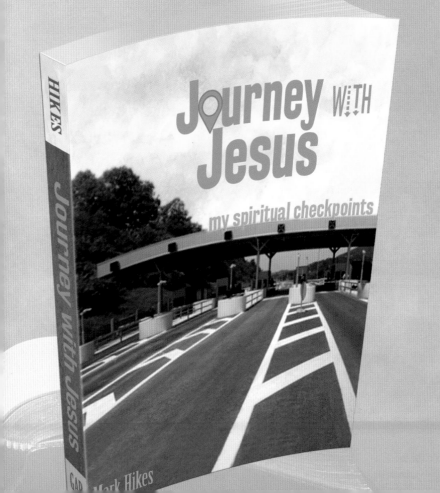

About the Author

Mark Hikes lives in Madison, Mississippi, with his wife, Natalie, and two sons, DJ and Jack. They share life with four rescue animals—three dogs, Yetti (Akita), Emma (Australian Shepherd), Maggie (Red Bone Coon Hound), and one cat, Charlie.

Mark lived most of his life in Central Pennsylvania where he was born and raised in the town of Pine Grove. He loves outdoor sports and discipleship time with family and small groups.

Mark is a member of Madison United Methodist Church where he serves as a Family Group Leader.

Thank you for reading the second book in the **15 MINUTES WITH JESUS SERIES**. My hope is that it will bring you, and others, closer to our Father. We should all really try to spend more time with Him!

I could never have imagined the number of phone calls and texts I received from the first book. I loved speaking to everyone that reached out to me. I'm extending the same invitation to you.

What was your favorite topic? What did it make you think about? How did it make you feel? Did it help you in some way?

Call, text or email me: **(717) 439-8575 or mhhikes@gmail.com**

Great American Publishers

Great American Publishers (Lena, MS) is a small press specializing in souvenir cookbooks.

Our tradition of preserving America's favorite recipes is celebrated in our state cookbook series. The **STATE HOMETOWN COOKBOOK SERIES** is a hometown taste of America featuring favorite recipes from home cooks along with sidebars about each state's fun food festivals.

The **STATE BACK ROAD RESTAURANT RECIPES SERIES** is a fun restaurant road trip featuring favorite recipes from chefs and restaurant owners along with profiles about the best locally owned restaurants to enjoy while traveling the state.

In addition to these two series and more, we publish a line of national favorite cookbooks, state specific notebooks, and Christian devotionals.

Call us toll-free for more information
1-888-854-5954

Visit us online
www.GreatAmericanPublishers.com

Connect with us on facebook
www.facebook.com/GreatAmericanPublishers

If you missed out on the first book in the series, be sure to check it out here: